# The Practitioner Inquiry Series

Marilyn Cochran-Smith and Susan L. Lytle, *SERIES EDITORS*

*(continued)*

# Building Racial and Cultural Competence in the Classroom

## Strategies from Urban Educators

Edited by

### KAREN MANHEIM TEEL
### JENNIFER E. OBIDAH

Teachers College, Columbia University
New York and London

Published by Teachers College Press, 1234 Amsterdam Avenue, New York, NY
10027

*Library of Congress Cataloging-in-Publication Data*

Building racial and cultural competence in the classroom : strategies from
    urban educators / edited by Karen Manheim Teel and Jennifer Obidah.
        p. cm.
    Includes bibliographical references and index.
    ISBN 978-0-8077-4861-9 (pbk. : alk. paper) —
    ISBN 978-0-8077-4862-6 (hardcover : alk. paper)
        1. Multicultural education—United States. 2. Race relations—Study and
    teaching—United States. 3. Culture—Study and teaching—United States.
    4. Teachers—In-service training—Social aspects—United States. I. Teel,
    Karen Manheim. II. Obidah, Jennifer E.
    LC1099.3.B845  2008
    370.1170973—dc22                                              2008000672

ISBN 978-0-8077-4861-9 (paper)
ISBN 978-0-8077-4862-6 (cloth)

Printed on acid-free paper
Manufactured in the United States of America

15  14  13  12  11  10  09  08        8  7  6  5  4  3  2  1

# Contents

*v*

# Building Racial and Cultural Competence in the Classroom

## Strategies from Urban Educators

# CHAPTER ONE

# Setting the Stage

*Karen Manheim Teel*
*Jennifer E. Obidah*

## HOW THIS BOOK CAME ABOUT

The original idea for this book came from Karen Teel's graduate students in her educational psychology course at Holy Names University in Oakland, California.

> At Holy Names University, where I teach and advise students in the single-subject credential program, the most important goal of our teacher education program is to prepare our students to teach successfully in urban settings. I want my students to understand the roles that personal and institutional racism play in low student achievement among students of color, and, in particular, African American students. I want to challenge their thinking as I was challenged by Jennifer Obidah and many others over the years.

Over the semester, many of Karen's students, who are predominantly White, begin to realize how little they know about the experience, history, and culture of their K–12 students of color and how important it is for them to examine their own roles in the struggles that many of their students experience around literacy issues, behavior conflicts with teachers, perceived irrelevant curriculum, and, consequently, disproportionately low achievement (Delpit, 1995/2006; Delpit & Dowdy, 2003; Gordon, 2000; Ladson-Billings, 1994, 2001). Some students say they have begun seeking guidance in examining their own racial/cultural stereotypes and biases. Others mention that they have rarely discussed issues of racism and racial and cultural inequities in any classes they have taken previously. Many of Karen's students of color tell her that in her classes they find their voices and experience being heard and validated in some cases for the first time, which others have written about as well (Delpit, 1995/2006; Epstein, 2006; Gordon, 2000). Karen states:

> Of all the readings I assign, the students find Lisa Delpit's *Other People's Children* (1995/2006) particularly useful and accessible. Because Delpit integrates her own story into her analysis, they find they not only listen to her, but are able to hear her. Many students want more readings like Delpit's, and also would like readings that represent alternatives to Delpit's perspective. They have asked if there are any anthologies written by a diverse group of educators that both further illuminate how to teach "other people's children" and also show how the authors' views about teaching emerged from their own experience. Jennifer and I compiled this book in response to their expressed need.

## OUR DEFINITION OF RACIAL AND CULTURAL COMPETENCE

We see this edited book as a tool to enhance what we are calling the "racial and cultural competence" of relatively new as well as veteran practicing teachers and teacher educators. Our definition of *racial and cultural competence* was largely influenced by the words of one of three writing teams, established by a state-appointed education board in Ohio (Senate Bill 2, Educator Standards Board, 2004).

The Educator Standards Board was charged with the responsibility of recommending standards for teachers, principals, and professional development; creating a definition of cultural competence; and integrating that definition throughout the standards.

Several members of the writing team in Ohio that worked on the standards for teachers created a definition of cultural competence and wove aspects of that definition into the narrative descriptions, elements, and indicators of their recommended standards. A member of this writing team—Fran Peterman, who was a professor at Cleveland State University—shared her writing team's definition with us at the time they were working on it. Her writing team described cultural competence as teachers' ability to

> see differences among students as assets. They create caring learning communities where individual and cultural heritages, including languages, are expressed and valued. They use cultural and individual knowledge about their students, their families, and their communities to design instructional strategies that build upon and link home and school experiences. They challenge stereotypes and intolerance. They serve as change agents by thinking and acting critically to address inequities distinguished by (but not limited to) race, language, culture, socioeconomics, family structures, and gender.
>
> Beyond using images, literature, and other forms of expression that represent students' diverse cultures and backgrounds, teachers understand, affirm, and use students' home and primary languages, communication styles, and family structures for learning and discipline.

This definition of cultural competence and the indicators that accompanied it appeared in ongoing drafts of the standards for Ohio educators, recommended by Fran's writing team. However, they do not appear in the final document adopted by the Ohio Board of Education in October 2005.

We were not aware of this development in Ohio when we began putting this book together, but we were so captured by the idea of cultural competence as an expectation for all teachers that we decided to make it an integral part of our book. As we reflected on the above definition, however, we shifted to racial and cultural competence, incorporating—as part of teacher competence—more focus on the inequities across both race and culture. As such, we added the concept of *power* to highlight the racial and cultural hierarchies that grow out of the institutional racism that exists in our society. We consider institutional racism to be the conscious or unconscious, systematic, institutionalized mistreatment of particular racial and ethnic groups.

We believe that developing racial and cultural competence needs to be an ongoing effort for all educators. This competence, in our opinion, is as important as competence in classroom management, curriculum, lesson planning and delivery, and assessment. In fact, all of those competencies should become stronger and stronger as a teacher becomes more and more racially and culturally competent.

Ultimately, and most importantly, teachers' awareness of race, of the possibility of their own racism and the racism of others, and the significance of these perceptions in the teaching and learning process are key factors that must be dealt with in the kind of teaching competence we advocate. In sum, we use the term *racial and cultural competence* to signal the importance of teachers' awareness of power imbalances in classrooms with respect to differences in race (their own and that of others) and culture wherein the White dominant culture is allowed most of the time to set up the winners as those who fit its mold. Racially and culturally competent teachers are willing and able to mediate such power imbalances by understanding, supporting, and advocating for students who historically have experienced "underachievement" in American schools.

## CONNECTIONS WITH THE ACHIEVEMENT GAP

Historically, in public schools in the United States, inner-city African American students have experienced disproportionate underachievement (Delpit, 1995/2006; Epstein, 2006; Ladson-Billings, 1994, 2001; Obidah & Teel, 2001; Perry, Steele, & Hilliard, 2004; Tatum, 1997). This often is referred to as the *achievement gap*. Although the challenge to reduce the achievement gap has been taken up by well-intentioned teachers and policymakers for decades, they have had only limited success. Recent results of a study (National Center for Education Statistics, 2007) show that the student population of color in the United States has increased dramatically over the past 30 years, from 22% of public school enrollment to 42%, and the achievement gap has not changed. One reason for this, in our view, is that since the end of desegregation, the teaching force has become increasingly White, and many of these White teachers (along with some teachers of color), are ill-prepared to work effectively with students of color in urban settings. Other writings have addressed this problem as well (Cochran-Smith, 2004; Delpit, 1995/2006; Epstein, 2006; Howard, 1999/2006; Obidah & Teel, 1996, 2001).

There are many ways to document the race and class achievement gap (perhaps more properly referred to by one of our chapter contributors, Ann Berlak, as the *opportunity gap*), including high school and college dropout and graduation rates and grades. However, the most commonly used indices are based on scores on standardized tests.

The Academic Performance Index (API), derived from student scores on standardized tests, is the most widely used index of school quality. Consistently, across school districts, the APIs of inner-city schools (with large African American student populations) are extremely low (1s & 2s), with top API levels (9s & 10s) scored by suburban schools with large White populations.

We think that personal and institutional racism contributes most significantly to this discrepancy. More specifically, we have observed many White teachers who know little about African American history and culture and have not had the opportunity to explore their own racist conditioning and its effects on their pedagogy. Both of these factors negatively influence the classroom environment, the relationship between teachers and students, teachers' expectations of their students, and students' willingness to apply themselves fully. We assert that these are the most significant in-school factors contributing to the achievement gap.

Teachers are not, of course, solely responsible for the gap. We must not discount the influences of inadequate health care, housing, school buildings, and student–teacher ratios, along with the inequitable distribution of qualified teachers and the lack of affordable child care for families with two minimum-wage workers who, together, do not earn a living wage. We often hear and read about other explanations for the achievement gap, such as lack of family support and peer and neighborhood issues. We assert, however, that educators who attribute the achievement gap solely to those life circumstances of their students outside of school are shirking their own responsibilities in schools to mentor and have high expectations for their students, many of whom consequently are failing.

Addressing these issues of racism and racial and cultural inequities is crucial to the success of African American students in particular. These issues should be grappled with continually in our schools and in teacher education programs across the country, whether or not credential students are being prepared to teach in urban settings. We are aware of only a handful of teacher education programs that include these issues as a major component. *Building Racial and Cultural Competence in the Classroom: Strategies from Urban Educators* presents the perspectives and experiences of 12 teachers and teacher educators who address these issues. Our hope is that each chapter will enhance the power of those educators who read it to promote both the school success of marginalized racial/ethnic groups and their students' understanding of cultural, social, and political inequities.

## COMPARISONS WITH EARLIER LITERATURE

There are many excellent books that address the impact of racial and cultural inequities on teaching and learning in urban schools (Berlak & Moyenda, 2001; Delpit, 1995/2006; Howard, 1999/2006; Ladson-Billings, 1994, 2001; Landsman, 2001; Obidah & Teel, 2001). These books as a group describe both effective and ineffective urban classroom teachers. However, the approach in our book is different in several unique ways. First, our book is told in 12 voices, whereas the earlier books typically written are by only one author. Second, with the exception of Berlak and Moyenda (2001) and Obidah and Teel (2001), the earlier books were written by either White authors or authors of color. In contrast, we are a team of authors of different racial and cultural backgrounds. This multiracial and multicultural perspective makes our book unique because not only does each of us offer a different racial/cultural perspective, but the reader may draw patterns of similarities and differences across our individual stories, which will further clarify our contrasting childhood and adulthood experiences that have influenced our thinking around these issues. Third, in every chapter, the authors have conceptualized and focused on an essential and always evolving way of being as educators in urban classrooms or in teacher education programs. This way of being manifests itself as racial and cultural competence. In this way, not only do we address, both philosophically and theoretically, the issues of racism and racial and cultural inequities, but we also give examples of practical ways to engage in successful, meaningful education for K–12 students of color.

## THEORETICAL UNDERPINNINGS

Two assumptions framed the issues we address in this book. The first is that the beliefs, intentions, and personalities of teachers play a more significant role in the success or failure of individual students than do the curriculum, materials, class size, or particular pedagogical skills that recently have been brought to center stage through scripted curricula and teacher performance assessments. We assert that the way of being that manifests itself in what we are calling racial and cultural competence is at the heart of successful teaching in urban settings (Ayers, 2001; Berlak & Moyenda, 2001; Cochran-Smith, 2004;

Delpit, 1995/2006; Epstein, 2006; Giroux, 1984; Gordon, 2000; Hale, 2001; Howard, 1999/2006; Kunjufu, 2002; Ladson-Billings, 1994, 2001; Landsman, 2001; Nieto, 1996/2004, 2007; Obidah & Teel, 2001; Perry, Steele, & Hilliard, 2004; Ramsey, 2004). From this perspective, as individual teachers transform their own racial and cultural understanding and attitudes, becoming racially and culturally competent, their teaching strategies will become more effective, their students' performance will improve, the institutions of schooling themselves will change, and the achievement gap will close.

The second assumption is that teachers' unconscious biases often undermine our consciously espoused intentions (Berlak & Moyenda, 2001; Blau, 2003; Boateng, 1990; Cummins, 1986; Hale, 2001; Howard, 1999/2006; Kunjufu, 2002; Landsman, 2001; Obidah & Teel, 2001; Perry, Steele, & Hilliard, 2004; Sleeter, 1994; Tatum, 1997). Thus, good intentions are not enough to counter the racism and racial and cultural inequities in American society. Because of their powerful potential to influence students' lives, all teachers, especially the largest group—middle-class White teachers—need to learn how to recognize the subtle biases in their own behavior, such as decisions they might make based on White privilege. They also need to help their students recognize their own racial and cultural biases. Addressing those subtle biases and capturing the essence of racial and cultural competence were the goals of this book.

## STRUCTURE OF THE BOOK

The stories recounted in *Building Racial and Cultural Competence in the Classroom* include each author's personal experiences either grappling with or being unaware of racism and racial and cultural inequities during a formative period in his or her life. Each chapter also includes concrete ideas about actions that practicing teachers and teacher educators might take to narrow the race and culture achievement gap. Some chapters analyze how these issues impact preservice teachers' abilities to teach inner-city African American students successfully; others focus on the struggles of teacher educators to illuminate these issues in their courses. *Although each chapter of our book addresses the topic of racism as the authors have experienced it, the experiences of the authors as educators, and suggestions for other educators; the order of the topics; and the nature of the personal accounts vary from chapter to chapter.*

Following are brief descriptions of each of the chapters. The order of the chapters was determined by their focus—with the teacher educator role coming first, followed by chapters describing classroom teaching experiences and the teacher educator role, and ending with a focus on exemplary work of classroom teachers with K–12 students.

Ann Berlak, in Chapter 2, lays out the theory of the adaptive unconscious. As part of her discussion of this theory, Ann gives examples, drawn from her experience as a teacher educator, a supervisor of student teachers, and a classroom teacher, of how the racial adaptive unconscious affects responses both in the foundations course she teaches and in elementary school classrooms. Ann also uses her own experiences growing up and the experiences students report in their journals and racial autobiographies to illuminate how the adaptive unconscious is shaped.

In Chapter 3, Edward Fergus engages the reader in a conversation on how racial and cultural competence must include a nuanced understanding of racial/ethnic identification as jointly constructed among individuals, others, and societal context. He presents this notion of racial/ethnic identification among Latinos through empirical accounts of how his Black Latino identification operates in schools.

Carl Grant raises a number of challenging themes in Chapter 4, including the connection between institutionalized racism and special education in schools, and the shortcomings of globalization in terms of the lack of attention education has received. Carl frames these challenges in terms of his own personal experience, his research, and his work in teacher education. He emphasizes the real need for teachers with racial and cultural competence, who are in an excellent position to have a positive impact on the current, problematic educational landscape.

In Chapter 5, co-editor Jennifer Obidah tells her story as a young Black woman, living and working in New York City and learning about racism. She then focuses on her students' moments of conflict as they become aware of issues of racism, inequity, power, and privilege while she works with them in their teacher education program. Jennifer is particularly interested in the impact of these moments of conflict on students' continued engagement and future commitment to equitably serving students who are different from them racially and culturally.

Using her parents and grandparents as role models, in Chapter 6, Kimberly Mayfield describes the history of African American education in the United States. She focuses on what current teachers in urban schools can learn from African American teachers in African American communities before desegregation. Kimberly describes her dissertation research, which explored racism in teacher education programs, and reflects on how her own racial and cultural competence has developed using the wisdom of African American educators who came before her.

Chapter 7 was written by Christine Sleeter. Christine examines the challenging process for White educators of learning to become racially and culturally competent and of becoming allies of African American students. Her perspective is that coming to realize that we live in a racist society in which White people benefit, whether or not they intend to do so, is highly uncomfortable and calls into question many taken-for-granted beliefs. Christine uses racial identity development as a theoretical framework and includes personal examples from her own life growing up and struggling to become a racially and culturally competent educator herself, both as an urban high school teacher as well as a university graduate education instructor.

In Chapter 8, Tarika Barrett and Pedro Noguera share insights about how their own experiences in the field of education have shaped their understanding of what it means to develop racial and cultural competence. Tarika describes her work with deaf and hard of hearing students, while Pedro discusses his work with students who have been written off as incorrigible and unteachable. They argue that arriving at a state of racial and cultural competence is never fully achievable but is a career-spanning journey. Other questions they raise address how educators can avoid the pitfalls of subscribing to racial and cultural stereotypes that guide how they interact with their students.

Chapter 9 is written by Jeffrey Duncan-Andrade. He has stated three goals for his chapter: (1) to provide a dynamic framework that defines and analyzes indicators of teachers in urban schools who demonstrate racial and cultural competence; (2) to provide concrete examples of these indicators in urban classrooms, explaining their relationship to increased achievement and student and teacher assessments; and (3) to propose policy, in the form of preservice and schoolwide conditions, that will make these indicators possible in more classrooms.

In Chapter 10, Kitty Kelly Epstein argues that the most important racial and cultural competence for White and other teachers is an understanding of the economic injustices embedded within the educational system and the important role that the overrepresentation of Whites in the teaching force has on that reality. Kitty argues that racial and cultural competence in the classroom is more likely to result from a willingness to engage in struggles outside the classroom against the broader injustices.

Karen Manheim Teel, the other co-editor of this book, focuses in Chapter 11 on her ongoing journey, as a White educator, toward racial and cultural competence. Karen recalls her upbringing, early years of teaching, courses in graduate school, and experience doing classroom research with urban students, which awakened her to the dark reality of her own racism. Karen also presents a conceptual framework for racial and cultural competence. She describes various criteria, with anecdotal examples of those who seem to already have this competence, those who need to learn it, and how to work toward acquiring it.

Chapter 12 is written by Sekani Moyenda, who describes her classroom teaching as an example of what racial and cultural competence looks like. She explores the challenges that have arisen because she has become an effective African American teacher with African American children. According to Sekani's perspective, her success is in direct conflict with the White dominant society—reflected in district school policy. Sekani has several suggestions for new and veteran teachers striving to acquire racial and cultural competence.

This anthology is a mosaic of voices intended to inspire and guide new and veteran teachers and teacher educators, regardless of their own racial/cultural backgrounds, to become more racially and culturally competent with students of marginalized races and cultures.

## REFERENCES

Ayers, P. (2001). *To teach: The journey of a teacher.* New York: Teachers College Press.

Berlak, A., & Moyenda, S. (2001). *Taking it personally: Racism in the classroom from kindergarten to college.* Philadelphia: Temple University Press.

Blau, J. R. (2003). *Race in the schools: Perpetuating white dominance?* Boulder, CO: Lynne Rienner Publishers.

Boateng, F. (1990). Combatting deculturalization of the African-American child in the public school system: A multi-cultural approach. In K. Lomotey (Ed.), *Going to school: The African-American experience* (pp. 73–84). Albany: State University of New York Press.

Cochran-Smith, M. (2004). *Walking the road: Race, diversity, and social justice.* New York: Teachers College Press.

Cummins, J. (1986). Empowering minority students: A framework for intervention. *Harvard Educational Review, 56*(1), 18-36.

Delpit, L. (2006). *Other people's children: Cultural conflict in the classroom.* New York: The New Press. (Original work published 1995)

Delpit, L., & Dowdy, J. K. (2003). *The skin that we speak.* New York: Norton.

Epstein, K. K. (2006). *A different view of urban schools: Civil rights, critical race theory and unexplored realities.* New York: Peter Lang.

Giroux, H. (1984). Public philosophy and the crisis of Education. *Harvard Educational Review, 54*(2), 186–194.

Gordon, J. (2000). *The color of teaching.* London: Routledge Falmer.

Hale, J. (2001). *Learning while black: Creating educational excellence for African American children.* Baltimore: Johns Hopkins University Press.

Howard, G. R. (2006). *We can't teach what we don't know: White teachers, multiracial schools.* New York: Teachers College Press. (Original work published 1999)

Kunjufu, J. (2002). *Black students/middle class teachers.* Self-published.

Ladson-Billings, G. (1994). *The dreamkeepers: Successful teachers of African American children.* San Francisco: Jossey-Bass.

Ladson-Billings, G. (2001). *Crossing over to Canaan.* San Francisco: Jossey-Bass.

Landsman, J. (2001). *A white teacher talks about race.* Lanham, MD: Scarecrow Press.

National Center for Education Statistics. (2007, June 1). U.S. data show rapid minority growth in school rolls. *New York Times.*

Nieto, S. (2007). *Affirming diversity: The sociopolitical context of multicultural education.* White Plains, NY: Longman. (Original work published 1996)

Obidah, J., & Teel, K. M. (1996). The impact of race and cultural differences on the student/teacher relationship: A collaborative classroom study by an African American and Caucasian teacher research team. *Kansas Association for Supervision and Curriculum Development Record, 14*(1), 70–87.

Obidah, J. E., & Teel, K. M. (2001). *Because of the kids: Facing racial and cultural differences in schools.* New York: Teachers College Press.

Perry, T., Steele, C., & Hilliard, A. (2004). *Young, black, and gifted.* Boston: Beacon Press.

Ramsey, P. (2004). *Teaching and learning in a diverse world.* New York: Teachers College Press.

Senate Bill 2, Education Standards Board, 2004.

Sleeter, C. (1994). White racism. *Multicultural Education, 1*(4), 5–8.

Tatum, B. D. (1997). *"Why are all the black kids sitting together in the cafeteria?" And other conversations about race.* New York: Basic Books.

# CHAPTER TWO

# Racial and Cultural Competence and the Adaptive Unconscious

*Ann Berlak*

## THE REALITY OF RACIAL INEQUALITY

All who grow up in the United States have, to varying degrees, come to take as given that people of color and their cultures are "less than." This message is transmitted by all the institutions of the society, including schools, the media, and the medical, legal, and political systems. All of us, White and of color, also receive the message that the lighter or whiter people's skin is, the better, smarter, more moral and deserving they are. Although we are rarely aware of it, institutional racism and White supremacy shape the value we all assign to both skin color and other markers of "race" and to the ethnic cultures of racial/ethnic groups. These processes perpetuate the tremendous degree of racial inequality in the United States today.

Neither I nor the preservice elementary school teachers I teach have escaped the effects of these powerful forces. In this chapter I first relate a story of my induction into the world of White (and Christian) supremacy growing up in St. Louis in the 1940s and 1950s. I then lay out the concept of the *adaptive unconscious* and consider how it illuminates what I have learned about involving students in the process of exploring how their racial identities and views of race were formed. I believe such explorations are essential if teachers are to become racially and culturally competent and thus able to contribute to the transformation of the racial order.

## HOW I LEARNED THAT LIGHT-SKINNED (AND CHRISTIAN) IS RIGHT AND DARK-SKINNED (AND JEWISH) IS "LESS THAN"

The eyes of 21 White children look out at me from a 62-year-old photograph of me and my 1st-grade classmates. We are seated at our desks in a spacious sun-filled room. We all look and are safe and well cared for. Dick and Jane and all the children in our readers are White, except for Little Black Sambo, and George Washington Carver, who we learn was a good man because he invented many uses for the peanut. Few of us have chores to perform at home, nor do our mothers do much cleaning or cooking. The "Negro" women who do the cooking and cleaning arrive at our houses on buses that (as I know now) have been scheduled for our parents' convenience. It is these dark-skinned women who, although some (I now realize) undoubtedly had children of their own, saw to it that *my* soiled laundry reappeared weekly, washed and ironed, in my closet and neatly arranged in my dresser drawers, and fed *my* appetite with aromatic yeast rolls and apple pies. They were the only dark-skinned people who ever spoke to me and to whom I ever spoke.

On dark and dreary St. Louis winter Saturdays, I and my White Christian schoolmates went to matinees at the Shady Oak, each feature preceded by a newsreel and a cartoon. In the darkened theater I watched cartoons that portrayed Black people as silly, stupid, and savage. The newsreels concerned themselves almost exclusively with decisions and actions of White Christian people (almost always men). The newsreel images of piled-up skeletons and emaciated bodies that greeted the liberators of the death camps that I saw when I was 8 years old were the only exceptions I remember. Although Jews of my parents' generation knew enough about anti-Semitism to have written tomes about it, the elders with whom I came into contact hardly spoke one word about it to us, their children.

I still have a one-page essay entitled "cotton" carefully printed in pencil that I wrote in 2nd grade. It reads in part:

> There are many states in which cotton is grown. . . . The cotton needs hot weather and moist ground. In the early spring there are pretty flowers. Then comes a brown boll. The cotton boll bursts. Cotton comes out. In the summer the cotton choppers come out and chop the cotton. The darkies do most of the work. If you see the cotton fields any time of the year you would think it is pretty!

Although I now know that "Negroes" were required to sit in separate sections of the movie theaters, and were not allowed in the "White" swimming pools, schools, or restaurants, I was not conscious of this then, nor did I give a second thought to why all the children in my school were White. On a family vacation in Florida when I was 10, I saw posted at a golf course "Colored" and "White" on the drinking fountains and noticed that only the "White" fountain had ice-cold water. This image has maintained its intensity for more than 50 years.

Although my family was Jewish, my most vivid holiday memories are of Christmas, not Passover, Hanukkah, or Rosh Hashanah. Fixed in my memory are the Christmas cards from my father's customers that accumulated on our mantelpiece, particularly the ones of snow-covered churches from whose windows streamed light that illuminated the sparkling snow. Gathering in the auditorium at school around the Christmas tree to sing familiar and glorious Christmas carols seemed to me pure bliss. Nothing at school acknowledged that Jews existed. I yearned to be but never was invited to Charlevoix, Michigan, by the "popular" and blond Judy Thompson, whom I considered my best friend, unaware that Jews were not welcome in Charlevoix.

Many years have passed since I yearned to be like and liked by the blond and Christian Judy Thompson, viewed African Americans as happy "Darkies" (using that term so unproblematically), and encountered White and Colored drinking fountains. Race, racism, and White supremacy have now become central issues in my life. I do not fully understand how the change occurred. There was no single moment when I suddenly saw myself through the eyes of African Americans or other people of color, or realized the opportunities that flowed from the privileges I received from being White. Rather, I see my increasing awareness as slow and uneven, stimulated in a myriad of small ways in part by my Jewish ethnic heritage. In high school I volunteered to participate in an interracial workshop sponsored by the National Conference of Christians and Jews (NCCJ). Perhaps I volunteered because the announcement of the workshop was the only time I had heard the word "Jews" used at school. I learned antiracist songs from a guitar-playing hippy head counselor at the NCCJ children's camp where I moved from the ranks of junior counselor to unit leader beginning at age 14. Perhaps being the only Jewish person (student or teacher) in my school throughout elementary school and junior high, hearing the story of the Jewish people's escape from slavery reiterated yearly on

Passover, and my discovery of *The Diary of Anne Frank* helped me construct the schema that enabled me to recognize the marginalization and dehumanization experienced by other groups of people. Perhaps my concern for racial justice flowed from contradictions I saw between the silences surrounding the "White" and "Colored" drinking fountains and the promises of liberty and justice for all that I repeated every day at school as I pledged allegiance to the flag in those sunny classrooms so many years ago.

In all my formal education, I never had one single teacher who asked me to reflect upon my conscious or unconscious views of race, racism, and White privilege, or to consider how the experience of those who were targeted by racism might differ from my own.

## THE PROBLEM:
## THE GAP BETWEEN CONSCIOUS COMMITMENTS AND PRACTICE

Early each semester I tell the story of Katie (all names in this chapter are pseudonyms), a White student who had made an "A" in the foundations of education course some years ago. The "A" signified, among other things, that Katie had explored the issue of racism thoughtfully, unlearned most aspects of her racist conditioning, and was well on her way to becoming an antiracist teacher and an ally to people of color. The semester following Katie's participation in my course, I became the supervisor of her student teaching. Within the first half hour of my first observation of her teaching, I watched this intelligent and committed young woman put the names of three misbehaving Black boys on the board while ignoring the identical behavior in several of the White boys. This event prompted me to ponder the contradiction between Katie's espoused beliefs and values and her behaviors. Although when I first saw Katie teach I became aware that I had failed her, I had no framework for thinking about what I could have done about it.

## MY FIRST ATTEMPT TO UNDERSTAND: RESISTANCE THEORY

In 2001 I co-authored with Sekani Moyenda a book called *Taking It Personally: Racism in the Classroom from Kindergarten to College*. In that book Sekani and I looked at my antiracist pedagogy and students' responses to it by focusing on a traumatic racially charged incident that occurred one day in class after Sekani, a Black 1st-grade teacher and former student in my foundations course, made a presentation to my class. I analyzed the event, its antecedents, and its consequences, using psychoanalytic concepts, primarily trauma, guilt, anxiety, fear, mourning, denial, repression, and resistance.

In spite of my analysis and my attempt to adjust my teaching in the wake of my new understandings, I knew that some students still left the course with little more than a superficial awareness of the stranglehold the racial hierarchy had on their hearts and minds. Take, for example, Sue, a White student. In her final journal entry she wrote, "The most profound changes that have taken place throughout the semester have been my attitudes about race. . . . I was one of those people who believed racism didn't exist." But in her final paper, also written at the end of the semester, she wrote:

> When I asked my master teacher about her thoughts about
> the achievement gap and the African American culture (single
> mothers, children from multiple fathers) she quickly corrected
> me that it wasn't about any particular culture or race since
> all races do care about their children. In no uncertain terms
> she (the master teacher) let me know it was all about socioeco-
> nomic status [not race]. I now realize this is true.

Apparently, in spite of our close, intense study of how institutional racism affects the families, school experience, and achievement of African American children, when all was said and done, and her protestations to the contrary, she still did not view the achievement gap (more properly referred to as the opportunity gap) through the lens of racism. Sue's blindness at the end of the course to the power of racism seemed an unwelcome repetition of some students' tenacious blindness we had explored in *Taking It Personally.*

My pedagogy, particularly after writing *Taking It Personally,* had been informed by an assumption I shared with others who look at antiracist teaching through a psychoanalytic lens, namely, that what and how students learn is influenced by an unconscious *resistance* to learning things that reveal the problematic nature of their beliefs.[1] In *Taking It Personally* I explored reasons for this unconscious resistance to acknowledging the racism that was palpable in students' responses to Sekani's presentation, as follows:

Perhaps the (White and Asian) students' fear of Sekani was an instance of unconscious but deeply engrained fear of encirclement by dark-skinned others. Perhaps they were associating Sekani with the terror they felt at the prospect of teaching a class populated by what they . . . had come to see as violence-prone Black children. . . . Maybe Jim [a White student] and the others resisted acknowledging Sekani's expertise because they were trying to maintain the floodgates that protected them against a dawning awareness that their positions in the racial hierarchy, which provided important sources of self esteem, were unearned and undeserved. (pp. 122–123)

A second understanding I drew from my analysis of Sekani's encounter with my class was that in order for some students to "hear" information that challenges their belief systems, they must experience emotional discomfort and disorientation or trauma. In *Taking It Personally* we documented that many students had experienced the encounter as traumatic. Before the session in which Sekani made her guest presentation was over, several students had broken into tears, angry tones of voice had reverberated down the hall, and one student had left the room abruptly. A White student later reported:

I'm still thinking of [Sekani's] visit. . . . I feel like my insides have been ripped out. . . . So far this has been my range of emotions: intimidation, rage, defensive attitude, hopelessness, guilt, confusion, hope, respect. . . . And I would say that's just the tip of the iceberg.

I knew that I could not fabricate each semester the trauma we experienced during Sekani's visit. Thus, I continued to ponder how to "get through" to more students at a deeper level.

## THE ADAPTIVE UNCONSCIOUS

As I was reflecting on these issues, I came upon Malcolm Gladwell's bestseller *Blink* (2004) and then read Tim Wilson's *Strangers to Ourselves: Discovering the Adaptive Unconscious* (2002), cited as a source by Gladwell. Wilson's intention was to integrate insight or depth psychology with the American traditions of cognitive and social psychology that I had been schooled in as a graduate student but had not followed for years. The theory of the adaptive unconscious Wilson and Gladwell set out suggested a new way for me to think about racism and the promotion of racial and cultural competence.

The central idea of the theory is that all people have two relatively independent information processing systems: the conscious and the adaptive unconscious. These two systems have evolved in different ways and serve different functions. The adaptive unconscious is far more sophisticated, efficient, and adult-like than the unconscious portrayed by psychoanalytic theory. It can set goals, interpret and evaluate evidence, and influence judgments, conscious feelings, and behavior. People can think in quite sophisticated ways and yet be thinking "nonconsciously." Wilson calls it the *adaptive* unconscious because it has evolved to enable human survival. It permits us to notice danger and to initiate behavior quickly.

Attitudes toward concepts such as race or gender, for example, operate at two levels—at a conscious level where our stated values direct our behavior deliberately, and at an unconscious level where we respond in terms of immediate but quite complex automatic associations that tumble out before we've even had time to think. Conscious thought takes a longer view; it is controlled and slow, and requires effort. As exemplified by Katie and Sue, these systems can incorporate diametrically opposed ways of interpreting experience, and vastly different feelings and motives that guide behavior. Many classroom studies have documented that the gap I observed between Katie's and Sue's conscious and unconscious views is not at all unique (e.g., Ferguson, 2000; Lewis, 2004).

Gladwell compares the adaptive unconscious to a giant computer that crunches all the data from all the experiences we have had. This collection of efficient, sophisticated, unconscious information processing systems that selects, interprets, and evaluates incoming information, directs our attention, filters our experience, and influences almost all of our second-by-second responses. Thus, the adaptive unconscious is much more influential in teachers' daily classroom performance than most of us are aware of, and we exert less control over our classroom actions than we imagine.

The adaptive unconscious operates almost entirely out of conscious view. So independent are the two systems that Gladwell characterizes the snap judgments or rapid cognitions characteristic of the adaptive unconscious as taking place behind a locked door. To use another metaphor, identifying aspects of the adaptive unconscious may be no easier than viewing the assembly language controlling our word processing computer program (Wilson, 2002).

However, there is compelling evidence that, although people's unconscious motives may be inaccessible to them, they rarely feel ignorant (Gladwell, 2004). Instead, asking people to explain why they acted as they did is likely to lead to fabrications that have nothing to do with and may even contradict their unconscious motivations (Wilson, 2002). We are likely to explain our actions by using first- and second-hand stories and testimonies from our experience that are consistent with the conscious cultural and personal, often "politically correct," theories that come most easily to mind (Wilson, 2002, p. 169); that is, the explanations that *are* accessible to consciousness. A woman may explain that her fear of Black men is the result of an individual psychological disposition that resulted from knowing someone who was raped by a Black man, rather than considering that long-established aspects of her adaptive unconscious may account better for her fears.

### Origins of the Racial Adaptive Unconscious

The adaptive unconscious is in part genetically determined: We are all prewired to fit experiences into categories. However, the *particular* categories we use are certainly not innate. They are fashioned and strengthened through repetition and frequent use, from the thousands of micro-messages our families and communities send us nonverbally as well as verbally, the books we've read, the media we've encountered, and our schooling experiences, including both the explicit and the hidden curriculum (e.g., racial patterning of the power hierarchies in schools, the subtexts in textbooks,[2] and racially coded tracking systems). In all these ways we learn to see color and to categorize people racially in terms of the array of categories the society we live in at the time offers us (see Chapter 3, this volume).

Paradoxically, although racial categories and hierarchies are deeply etched in almost all of us almost from birth, teachers' and the media's virtual silence about racism ensures that most White people and some people of color will not recognize racism even when it is right before our eyes. The blindness is enabled in part by multi-faceted and ubiquitous messages of meritocracy: that it is those who work hard who "make it" (and the corollary that those who didn't make it did not work hard). Although teachers may admonish individual acts of racist name-calling, and during Black History month or on Martin Luther King's birthday may discuss racism as interpersonal prejudice that occurred mostly in the past, they rarely acknowledge the historical and ongoing systematic institutionalized processes that are the heart of racism (see Chapter 7, this volume). Of course, most of us have no idea what these experiences are teaching us; the construction of our racial adaptive unconscious is beyond our control. That four White police officers, "thinking" he was about to shoot them, decimated the dark-skinned Amadou Diallo with a total of 41 bullets as he reached into his pocket to locate identification papers one winter night in the South Bronx is evidence of the potential destructiveness of the adaptive unconscious.

Because they have been subjected to the same messages that Whites have, people of color may develop and pass down perceptions that automatically and unconsciously position *themselves* and other people of color as "less than." On the other hand, they may learn a set of categories that positions European Americans as racists. In the latter case, as I often tell White students, people of color may well consider White people guilty of racism unless or until they are proven innocent.

## Accessing Our Adaptive Unconscious

In spite of the difficulties of finding out what is going on behind the locked door, it is not impossible to do so. Wilson (2002) suggests that one way we can learn about it is to make guesses or inferences about our adaptive unconscious from observing our own behavior. Another way to find out more is to pay close attention to what others think of us and to consider using that information to revise our beliefs about ourselves, even if this means adopting a more negative view of our behavior and its unconscious determinants.

Of course, using others' views of us as clues to our adaptive unconscious presents difficulties. To utilize this source of information about ourselves, we first would need to know what others *really* think of us, and others often hide their true views and impressions of us, particularly if these are critical. Sekani spent a semester as a student in my classroom without letting her classmates know that she was hearing many of their comments as racist. In addition, when others give us signals about what they really think, we often have a hard time receiving them (Wilson, 2002); our unconscious filters may protect us from negative feedback in order to enhance our sense of well-being.

## PROMOTING TEACHERS' RACIAL
## AND CULTURAL COMPETENCE

How can viewing classroom practice through the lens of the adaptive unconscious contribute to racial and cultural competence? Teachers are not normally taught to think about the origins and the effects on students of our first impressions and habitual reactions. The significance of the racial adaptive unconscious is more likely to be acknowledged in training programs for the police. As the recent shooting by members of the New York City Police Department of the unarmed and Black Sean Bell on the day of his wedding reminds us, the racial adaptive unconscious can be a matter of life and death. Catastrophic racial interactions that spring from the adaptive unconscious of teachers may not be as visible, newsworthy, and immediate as those of the police. However, they also may, ultimately, be matters of life and death. As Fergus (Chapter 3, this volume) argues, destruction of the self-esteem of children of color is far more devastating than their failure to learn to read and write.

The good news is that our unconscious thinking is in one critical respect no different from our conscious thinking: Both can change (Gladwell, 2004). This means we have to take the adaptive unconscious seriously and then take steps to understand and to alter or re-educate it.

### Teaching Credential Students About the Adaptive Unconscious

I am now exploring how thinking in terms of the adaptive unconscious can help me promote racial and cultural competence. I begin the first day of class by asking students to introduce themselves in terms of the racial/ethnic composition and tracking patterns of their elementary and high schools, and where they were positioned within these patterns. (The vast majority have never thought about this.) Then I lay out the basic elements of the theory and ask students to hypothesize what effect these early school experiences might have had on their unconscious views of race, class, culture, and opportunity: Whom were they learning through the hidden curriculum to categorize as smart and whom as dumb? Whose ethnic cultures were they learning to value and admire?

This initiates a process of teaching that I now conceptualize as an effort to affect the deep structures of students' adaptive unconscious, structures that are the most significant aspects of what educators often refer to as "prior knowledge." I want students to consider that their adaptive unconscious—the prior knowledge or assumptions that, without their awareness, motivate their behavior—may have a more profound effect on their teaching than theories they have learned or will learn in their courses and have conscious access to.

## Teaching as Building and Strengthening Selected Lenses

Each of us has a variety of automatic category systems we use to screen the data we encounter. Which one we will use at any particular moment to make sense of our experience depends on several factors. One is whether and how often the category system has been used in the past. Constructing or strengthening lenses requires time (in fact, a lifetime) and frequent repetitions. The experience of June, a White woman who never spoke up during the first 6 weeks of class, illustrates this process. Although we had already discussed and read and seen videos about racism during the two previous classes, it was only after viewing *The Color of Fear*, a film that shows a racially diverse group of men engaging emotionally with one another about racism, that June for the first time was able to grasp the significance of racism. In her final journal entry she described her growing awareness as follows:

> Most of what I learned (in the entire class) had to do with racism. . . . One thing I learned about was White privilege. I had heard the term in class but I had no idea how deep and pervasive it was, even after we did the White privilege exercise. When we watched *The Color of Fear* I saw how David didn't see how the non-Whites experienced racism, and I heard what the non-Whites had to say about their experiences with racism. Combined with the White privilege exercise it made a powerful impression on me. This made me re-think everything else we'd talked about on the subject of racism and finally shed a light that I had been lacking.

John's final journal entry also suggests the important role repetition can play.

> My refusal to dismiss the myth that "One will make it as long as she/he works hard" was certainly a high hurdle to conquer. . . . This might explain the persistence of my initial judgment against affirmative action (during the last week of class). I

guess I had continued to assume everyone was granted the same resources and placed at the same starting points even though as I now realize we had been thinking critically about this view all along.

Another example is the journal entry written by Lisa, a Chinese immigrant, describing the tenacity of a lens that normalizes White privilege.

The biggest accomplishment [that] emerged from this experience (the course) for me. . . . is my realization that I've internalized so many concepts that were essentially unhealthy to my overall well-being. The reason I did not see myself as a victim under racism was . . . I somehow welcomed the notion that White equates [with] superiority without registering [this] consciously. It was the most difficult step in this self-discovery journey for me. . . . I understand it must be a great challenge to overwrite [sic] much internalization that had been rooted in our minds and bring the subconscious to the surface.

I now realize that the disproportionate time I spend addressing racism—in contrast to classism and sexism and Euro-centrism—is a result of my understanding that, although each of these lenses is of equal and crucial importance, changing even one deep and fundamental structure of the mind within a 45-hour course is hard—certainly for some students impossible—to do. Spending equal time on all the issues would have a significant impact on none. It is not until students have developed lenses for recognizing specific instances of institutionalized racism and how it has shaped their adaptive unconscious, and thus their classroom behavior, that they can exercise racial and cultural competence.

Framing racial and cultural competence in terms of the adaptive unconscious also brings more clearly into focus the importance of teaching an antibias curriculum to very young children at the very time when their lenses are in the process of being formed (Van Ausdale & Feagin, 2001).

## Making Better Inferences About Our Adaptive Unconscious

How can we uncover our unconscious thoughts and attitudes, particularly the negative stereotypical automatic and unintentional aspects of our adaptive unconscious that may contradict our conscious understanding of ourselves? The first step is to learn to habitually, consciously, and deliberately analyze our behaviors for clues to our unconscious racial/cultural lenses, paying special attention to the pitfalls into which we know from social research we are likely to fall.

One classroom activity that provides an opportunity for students to make inferences about racialized elements of their adaptive unconscious occurs at the beginning of our focus on race and racism in classrooms. The activity focuses on students' responses to a video clip, a 3-minute excerpt from *School Colors*, a documentary about Berkeley High. I precede the clip with a part of *School Colors* that shows Black students discussing clear and compelling instances of racism they have experienced at Berkeley High. The clip shows a disciplinary conference attended by Jeff—a Black student at Berkeley High—and two White men, a teacher and a guidance counselor. Jeff is wearing a hooded sweatshirt and sunglasses. He has already been suspended. He tells the two White men that he came upon two female friends of his who were fighting in the hall and decided to take responsibility for breaking up the fight so his friends wouldn't get in trouble. The White teacher—whom Jeff had never seen before—grabbed Jeff, assuming he was going to join the fight. When grabbed by the White stranger, Jeff said to him, "If you touch me again I'm going to phuck you up." The teacher and the guidance counselor reiterate that Jeff has been suspended for threatening a teacher. Later in the scene Jeff tells the two men that he was issuing a warning and not a threat: "If you look in your dictionary, you'll see the difference. 'If you touch me again' is a warning; 'I'm going to phuck you up' is a threat. In my language that's spelled P-H-U-C-K." He also tells them that in his culture, "if a man grabs you who you do not know, you defend yourself," and that if he had not been on school grounds he would have hit any stranger who put his hands on him. After Jeff has left the room, the White men commiserate that they don't think Jeff really heard anything they said.

Next I ask the students to do a "quick write" about what they saw happening in the disciplinary scene, and how well they think the adults handled it. I then collect and redistribute the writings so that each student reads aloud what another has written and no one knows whose view is being spoken. In the class discussion that follows the "read-around," a variety of views are expressed. About half the students endorse the suspension and the adults' handling of the situation. ("At least Jeff had the opportunity to tell his side.") Another common view is that there were cultural differences between Jeff and the two men. Rarely does even a single student acknowledge the racial/cultural power differences and see the scene in terms of a racial power hierarchy where White people were in positions to make, apply, and enforce school rules.

We then discuss what inferences they might make, from their responses to the clip, about their racial adaptive unconscious. We also consider what can be inferred about the tenacity of their lenses from the fact that—in spite of viewing the Black students' discussion about the racism they experienced at the high school—they did not acknowledge any racial dimensions of the hearing. We also make inferences about the adaptive unconscious of those few (anonymous) students who thought Jeff had hit the teacher, although there is absolutely no evidence that he had done so (Steele & Aronson, 1995).

Thinking in terms of the adaptive unconscious has prompted me to refocus the racial autobiography assignment, which I have felt rarely got to the heart of the matter and have been dissatisfied with for years. Since I have come to think about racial autobiographies as narratives that trace the development of the racial adaptive unconscious as well as conscious racial feelings and beliefs, I now ask students to begin their autobiographies by describing both their conscious and unconscious racial views. I ask them to identify unconscious views by making inferences from their responses to the *School Colors* video clip and their response to Gloria Yamato's essay, "Something About the Subject Makes It Hard to Name" (1998). The essay categorizes all White people into four categories of racists, including "unaware/unintentional racists" and "unaware/self-righteous racists," and also explores internalized racism of people of color. I ask the students to look at themselves through Yamato's eyes and consider what doing so suggests to them about their own adaptive unconscious.

## CONCLUSION

Just because something is out of awareness doesn't mean it is out of control. The more aware teachers and teacher educators become of how structural hierarchies of race and ethnicity inhabit their adaptive unconscious and dictate their teaching behavior, the more likely they are to bring their actions into line with their conscious values and commitments. There appears to be some consensus that people sometimes can restrain their automatic responses, given ample knowledge about the dynamics that inform their behavior, the opportunity, and the (conscious) motivation (Payne, Lambert, & Jacoby, 2002). We can learn to be especially vigilant of our "gut feelings" in situations where we are required to act quickly or are under stress. We can learn to wait a beat before responding to first impressions or challenging situations, particularly when we have a hunch that elements of our adaptive unconscious are not in sync with our conscious beliefs and intentions.

Teachers' racial and cultural incompetence is not simply a consequence of a poor fit between the cultures of students and their teachers that flows from teachers' limited knowledge about the ethnic aspects of the cultures of children who are different from themselves. Difference in itself is not the problem. The problem is the racial and ethnic/cultural hierarchies that prospective teachers have internalized, particularly those that inhabit the adaptive unconscious.

Once we identify aspects of the adaptive unconscious that we hope to change, we can take active steps to manage and control the images and experiences with which we interact (Wilson, 2002). The vast majority of teachers want to be fair and just and to contribute to the construction of a more just and joyful future. But racial and cultural competence requires more than conscious knowledge and conscious good intentions.

## NOTES

1. See, for example, Kevin Kumashiro (2000, 2002)
2. An example of a subtext that I use in class to demonstrate the subtle ways in which people of color may be positioned as inhuman is taken from a history textbook. The passage reads as follows: "Many people in the South thought they had to have their slaves to produce their main crop, cotton." There is rarely a single student of any race who initially identifies how this passage dehumanizes enslaved people.

## REFERENCES

Berlak, A., & Moyenda, S. (2001). *Taking it personally: Racism in the classroom from kindergarten to college.* Philadelphia: Temple University Press.
Ferguson, A. (2000). *Bad boys: Public schools in the making of black masculinity.* Ann Arbor: University of Michigan Press.
Frank, A. (1952). *The diary of Anne Frank.* Garden City, NY: Doubleday.

Gladwell, M. (2004). *Blink: The power of thinking without thinking.* New York: Little, Brown.

Kumashiro, K. (2000). Toward a theory of anti-oppressive education. *Review of Educational Research, 70*(1), 25–53.

Kumashiro, K. (2002). Against repetition: Addressing resistance to anti-oppressive change in the practices of learning, teaching, supervising, and researching. *Harvard Educational Review, 72*(1), 67–92.

Lewis, A. (2004). *Race in the schoolyard: Negotiating the color line in classrooms and communities.* New Brunswick, NJ: Rutgers University Press.

Payne, B. K., Lambert, A. J., & Jacoby, L. L. (2002). Best laid plans: Effects of goals in accessibility bias and cognitive control in race-based mispercep-tions. *Journal of Experimental Social Psychology, 38,* 384–396.

Steele, C., & Aronson, J. (1995). Stereotype threat and intellectual test perfor-mance of African Americans. *Journal of Personality and Social Psychology, 69*(5), 797–811.

Van Ausdale, D., & Feagin, J. (2001) *The first R: How children learn race and racism.* New York: Rowman & Littlefield.

Wilson, T. (2002). *Strangers to ourselves: Discovering the adaptive unconscious.* Cambridge, MA: Harvard University Press.

Yamato, G. (1998). Something about the subject makes it hard to name. In M. L. Anderson & P. H. Collins (Eds.), *Race, class and gender* (pp. 71–76). New York: Wadsworth.

# CHAPTER THREE

# Being a Black Latino: Understanding the Significance of Racial/Ethnic Identification in Racial and Cultural Competence

*Edward Fergus*

## RACIAL/ETHNIC IDENTIFICATION AMONG LATINOS

At the onset of the 21st century, the public discourse on Latinos warned of the pending growth in this population by 2050. This anticipated population growth spurred a myriad of questions: Where are they located? How are they integrating or adapting in the United States? Are they learning English? Are they legal? These and other such questions are premised on a commonly held notion—we know who *is* Latino. According to the 2000 Census, over 35 million Latinos are living in the United States, and the mid-decade estimates document over 41 million Latinos. This population distribution includes over 900,000 (2.7%) who self-identify as Black Hispanic and 17.6 million (47.9%) as White Hispanic (Logan, 2003). This variation among Latinos exists across several national groups, but is more pronounced among certain groups. Black Hispanic as an identification is most prominent among Dominicans (12.7%), followed by Puerto Ricans (8.2%), Cubans (4.7%), and finally Central Americans (4.1%) (Logan, 2003). On the other hand, White Hispanic identification is most prevalent among Cubans (85.4%), followed by South Americans (61.1%), Mexicans (49.3%), and then Puerto Ricans (49%).

Concerning educational and social outcomes, the educational attainment of Black Hispanics is higher than that of White Hispanics (a mean 11.7 years versus 10.5 years); however, Black Hispanics have a lower median income, higher unemployment, and higher poverty rates than White Hispanics (Logan, 2003). These differences also are noted in studies on skin color and labor-market participation (Espino & Franz, 2002), and political activities and attitudes (Hochschild, Burch, & Weaver, 2005). Overall, this difference in identification and correlation to academic and social outcomes highlights what we don't talk about regarding Latinos—that is, stratification by skin color.

In our current school context, educators are challenged to understand the U.S. racial landscape and what it means to teach linguistically and culturally diverse students. However, educators are using their own paradigms of what race is, which is usually a White–Black hierarchy, to situate Latinos. In some regions of the country the hierarchy is White, Hispanic/Mexican, and Black. We have not inserted into the racial and cultural competence or racial/cultural responsive conversation what it means to construct a racial/ethnic identification among the fastest-growing ethnic minority group. What racial/ethnic categorization do Latinos want? What racial/ethnic categorization do we situate them in?

This chapter engages in a conversation on how racial and cultural competence must include a nuanced understanding of racial/ethnic identification as jointly constructed among individuals, others, and societal context. I present this notion of racial/ethnic identification among Latinos through personal accounts of how my Black Latino identification operates in schools as well as my research on Latinos of different skin color. In addition, I discuss the research on racial/ethnic identification and its significance for educators seeking to begin the continuous process of developing racial and cultural competence.

## LATINOS AND SKIN COLOR:
## A PERSONAL ACCOUNT

As a second- or 1.5-generation Black Latino, my schooling and immigrant adaptation experiences have been closely connected. The soundtrack to my life has always been, "How can you be Black and speak

Spanish?" This comment has become synonymous with reductionist behavior in the United States. In the United States and other western hemisphere countries, racial categories are prescribed with specific markers that include skin color, language, cultural attributes, hair texture, and so on. It is these markers that satisfy our need to categorize individuals in order to determine the ways in which to engage them. However, what happens when we encounter in the same person two body markers generally ascribed to different racial/ethnic groups? For example, Chinese individuals who speak Spanish and identify as Chino-Latino; East Indians who identify as Guyanese or Jamaican; and Blacks who speak Spanish and identify as Mexican. In these instances, we experience a dissonance between our self-constructed racial world and this new body. How do we situate? What marker takes precedence?

In 1983, I arrived in the United States as a 9-year-old worried about how I would survive in a context that did not include my *tías* and *tíos*, *primas* and *primos*, *abuelos*, and, most importantly, mi *país*. My first encounter involved my 3rd-grade teacher, who asked my name on the first day, and I replied "Eduar." (Officially my English-translated birth certificate says Edward, but my entire family has always called me Eduar or Eduardo.) My 3rd-grade teacher replied, "No, I won't call you that; you can choose either Eddie or Ed." Before coming to the United States, I watched a lot of American television, which I credit for helping me to understand American cultural cues and language; one of the many shows I saw was Mr. Ed. Thus, at that moment in the 3rd grade, my teacher was asking whether I wanted to be named after a horse; and of course I chose Eddie. Since that moment, I've recognized the power others have in naming who you are because of how they elect to situate your racial/ethnic identification and the extent to which they are willing to be responsive.

To this day, I am Eddie to most of the English-speaking world and Eduar/Eduardo to my family and friends. Our students continuously make decisions as to how they will represent themselves to their teachers. However, our practice as educators and individuals is to racially identify our students into the categories we find familiar and comfortable. But the question for racially and culturally competent practitioners is: How often is our categorization accurate? Do we jointly construct racial/ethnic identifications with our students or is it a unidirectional experience?

## MY RESEARCH

The limited research on the significance of skin color in the racial/ethnic identification of Latino students became the initial impetus for my dissertation work on phenotypically different Mexican and Puerto Rican students (Fergus, 2002, 2004). It was through this research that I was able to explore the dimensions of how Latino students interpreted external perceptions of their racial/ethnic identification and what that meant to them. When I asked the students about whether their teachers or peers had ever identified them as something different than Mexican or Puerto Rican, many replied yes.

> *Laura:* Yeah. People always ask me if I have Black in me and stuff, or, if I'm White and Mexican and stuff. I'm like, nah, I'm Puerto Rican, you know. They think, cause the way I act and talk that I'm a different race. But I'm not.
>
> *Nori:* Yeah, when I had grey contacts lot of people thought I was a White boy.
>
> *Interviewer:* Why did you have grey contacts?
>
> *Nori:* I just wanted to see how they looked.
>
> *Interviewer:* Did they think you were White just because of the contacts?
>
> *Nori:* Yeah and cause I have white skin.
>
> *Keyla:* They think I'm Puerto Rican because of the way Puerto Rican girls are figured; they say I have a Puerto Rican figure and my hair, the way I talk, and my light skin.
>
> *Mellie:* Um, yeah they thought I was Mexican. Because we had a Puerto Rican festival and they, you know I had a Puerto Rican flag and they look at me and say, Are you Puerto Rican?, and I say yeah, and they say, you don't look like it, you look Mexican or you look American or you look like . . . I'm like no. So they think of me as something else.

What I learned from this research is that the construction of race/ethnicity is simultaneously a process that involves self-defined notions of what ethnicity and race are, and a process engendered by external notions of ethnicity and race. That is, how these students thought of themselves, and what identification they could use, sometimes took into consideration how they were being read by others. These students could not simply be Mexican, Chicano, Boricua, or Puerto Rican. They were simultaneously White-looking, Black/biracial-looking, or Mexican/Hispanic-looking to others, and these external labels meant something to their African American peers and teachers.

For instance, the White-looking students were positioned according to their skin color and behavior. They were situated into a White-looking identification either through congruence or affiliation. Being affiliated with or having features that were congruent with those of Whites placed these students in situations in which they were either treated as White or at times made to feel as if they did not readily belong to a Mexican or Puerto Rican community. In order to offset their light skin color, many of the students identified themselves as Mexican or Puerto Rican. These identifications represented the students' way of positioning themselves within the racializing process. However, this self-positioning did not supersede the external interpretations of skin color. Thus, what emerged was a story of racializing that involved others positioning these students as either affiliated with or congruent with Whites, and these White-looking students challenging such racializing by positioning themselves into a Mexican or Puerto Rican category through artifacts and cultural events.

On the other hand, the Mexican/Hispanic-looking and Black/biracial-looking students were situated into racial and ethnic groups that were somewhat connected to their ethnic identification. The Mexican/Hispanic-looking students were situated as racially affiliated with Mexicans. The Black/biracial students were racially congruent with Blacks but not necessarily deemed as affiliated with Blacks. The Mexican/Hispanic-looking students contended with being situated as part of a collective term that others used as code for Mexican.

The Black/biracial-looking students experienced a similar kind of racializing. The students identified as such were Puerto Rican. Thus, it was plausible for them to stretch their Puerto Rican identification to include Black because, as many of them stated, part of Puerto Rico's cultural history includes a significant African presence. However, by being positioned as Black/biracial-looking in predominantly African American high schools, these students either donned or were perceived as having a Black persona. This impression of a Black persona solidified their affiliation with Blacks. Overall, neither category allowed for the students to be Mexican or Puerto Rican. Many of the students incorporated these labels into their repertoire of identities, but they could not eliminate such identities.

## MY LIVED EXPERIENCES WITH RACIALIZATION

In our U.S. racial landscape (as the students in my study illustrated), skin color is the inescapable marker, or as Stuart Hall (1990) calls it, the "floating signifier," that we utilize to reduce individuals to racial/ethnic categories. Before coming to the United States, I was in an American military school from 1st to 3rd grades. Thus, by the time we landed in the United States and I resumed 3rd grade, I had tested out of ESL classes. I remember being very thankful for not having to go back to the trailers—the type of trailers to which many schools today relegate the groups of students they consider marginal (e.g., students with special needs).

By the time I began 4th grade at a school in a suburb north of Chicago, I had gained enough proficiency in academic English that my teacher asked me to translate content for the two limited English proficient Mexican students in our class. These two students did not speak English, and the school apparently did not have an ESL teacher because they never left the class. It was in such instances that my native language became a tool of instruction for the classroom teacher, but, more important, I was conveniently situated as Latino, but still Black.

Between 8th and 12th grades I was the only Latino or Panamanian in my Spanish classes and I was affectionately renamed "Platanos." However, outside of that class I was perceived differently, as evidenced by one 10th-grade teacher's comment: "You're such a smart Black kid." This racial/ethnic affiliation continued in 11th grade, as indicated by my social studies teacher's comment: "I'm recommending you to AP history; you're a smart enough Black kid." Again, when I was an undergraduate, a faculty member stated, "I enjoy having you in class because you don't make us feel bad when we talk about race." Finally, in graduate school another faculty member stated, "How can you be Black and speak Spanish?"

These lived experiences of racialization reflect the perceived notions of teachers regarding my racial/ethnic affiliation, as well as their expectations based on my skin color. The intertwined nature of perceived racial/ethnic affiliation and expectations is an unquantifiable feature of the schooling process that Black and Latino students have to endure. For many students of color, over time these comments become the expected norm when interacting with White teachers. It's an unfortunate reality that is the basis for the protective posturing Black and Latino students will do inside the classroom because they have no sense of whether their teacher will create a classroom that engenders cultural safety (I discuss this concept later in the chapter).

An understanding of the significance of how skin color and power function in the racial/ethnic identification process must begin with a working knowledge of the functioning of that process. The next section provides a cursory overview of how racial/ethnic identification is constructed and how this knowledge has significance in building racial and cultural competence when working with Latinos.

## UNDERSTANDING IDENTITY CONSTRUCTION
## AS PART OF RACIAL AND CULTURAL COMPETENCE

Whenever I begin conversations with educators, particularly Whites, on culture and race, I ask about definition: What does it mean to be Black, White, Latino, and so on? In society? In your school? A common response I get from White educators is, "I never thought about my Whiteness or being White." This acknowledgment situates their privilege but also reifies for Whites that the construct of racial/ethnic identification (i.e., internal and external) is for "other people's children" and not for them. This dilemma in schools plays out time and time again with White teachers who are unable to understand how their defining themselves as not having to think about Whiteness situates their students of color as the different ones. Racial and cultural competence must include an understanding of how we construct racial/ethnic identification.

Let's begin with unpacking what it means to construct a racial/ethnic identification. For over 50 years sociologists have discussed the construction of racial and ethnic identification and its persistence as a result of culture, tradition, nation- or state-imposed ethnic categories, and external perceptions of identity (Barth, 1969; Glazer & Moynihan, 1970; Gordon, 1961; Nagel, 1986, 1994; Omi & Winant, 1994; Padilla, 1985; Patterson, 1975; Yancey, Ericksen, & Richard, 1976).

Research on racial/ethnic identification has endured various shifts. However, the most significant changes have been based on the assertion that the fundamental process of racial/ethnic identity formation involves boundary construction (Cornell, 1996). That is, as Fredrik Barth (1969) introduced, boundary construction is about who is in and who is out. This research emphasized what is involved in the construction of the boundary. In other words, how do we decide who is Black, Latino, or White? How do we decide who is not?

A good example of this boundary construction is the public construction of Tiger Woods as the "best Black golfer," even though he has constructed himself as a multiracial individual. The consumption of the boundaries of race and ethnicity by the public rests on specific markers, and Tiger's skin color became a giveaway and inevitably the only marker that mattered. Similarly, Sammy Sosa, who spoke with an accent and preferred to speak in Spanish, was noted intermittently for his Blackness, but not acknowledged for his Latinoness.

Over time, research on racial/ethnic boundary construction separated into two lines: (1) the situational or contextual factors that construct racial/ethnic cohesion and affiliation, and (2) the individual agency or choice that racial/ethnic groups have in the shaping and reshaping of racial/ethnic boundaries (Cornell, 1996). The first line of research considers "the societal conditions and resultant positional interests that have encouraged, compelled, or inhibited organization along ethnic boundaries . . . and thereby give logic to ethnic group formation and persistence" (Cornell, 1996, p. 266).

What is important for educators to know from this research is that racial/ethnic identification is intimately bound to and constructed from societal and material conditions. In other words, racial/ethnic groups develop from shared "material interests" (e.g., politics, language, culture), which themselves are constructed from specific historical circumstances or contexts (e.g., migration, community shifts, economic conditions, national or state policies). Additionally, as circumstances and/or contexts change, the material interests that constitute the racial/ethnic identification change and eventually alter the racial/ethnic boundary of the identity (Cornell, 1996).

The development of pan-ethnic labels, such as Asian, Latino/ Hispanic, and Native American, serves as a key example of how political, social, and economic contexts construct and shift the boundaries of identity. Pan-ethnic labels have grown out of a political and economic need to name or lump various groups into one category, with the expressed need to treat them similarly. However, the use of pan-ethnic labels by educators, in particular, not only places a label on an individual, but also designates a perceived understanding of a group. That is, labeling a student as Asian versus Chinese, or Latino versus Ecuadorian, or Native American versus Sioux Indian, creates vastly different constructs. Understanding the construction of racial/ethnic identification demands knowing that such labels as Black, Asian, and Hispanic/Latino situate a presumption of their cultural attributes; it's almost as if once we say Black or Latino, there is nothing else that we need to know. Overall, the significance of this research is to confirm that society has played an intimate role in constructing these pan-ethnic labels, and these actions have shaped the ways in which people view themselves, their place in the world, and the identities they can choose (Cornell, 1996).

Although the larger society has played a significant role in the construction of racial/ethnic identity, another line of research argues that individuals also play an active role in identifying themselves. More specifically, researchers in this area explore how individuals can make their own decisions about their racial/ethnic identity. This research highlights that individuals carry a portfolio of identities that they choose to use at their discretion. For example, in a Black context I assert my Black identity, while in a Latino context I assert my Latino identity. In a Panamanian context I assert my city identity, and in a White context I most often assert a Black identity.

The fluidity in shifting identity among Latinos, specifically, lies in the salience of race, ethnicity, and national origin. Numerous Latino authors have written about their experiences carrying this portfolio of identities and note the uniqueness of constructing these various identities with different audiences. However, what is important to note is that the content of this portfolio of identities is shaped in part by the social context. That is, racial/ethnic identity also operates as mandatory (Bashi, 1998; Cornell, 1988; Portes & MacLeod, 1996). In other words, an individual's racial/ethnic identification is constructed by both internal choice and outside agents' perceptions of that identity (Nagel, 1994; Saenz & Aguirre, 1991). For instance, identity functions differently among White Americans and Americans of African ancestry: "White Americans have considerable latitude in choosing ethnic identities . . . Americans of African ancestry, on the other hand, are confronted with essentially one ethnic option—Black" (Nagel, 1994, p. 156).

Such difference in the latitude of ethnic options demonstrates the boundary of identity and the significant role outside agents play in restricting the available options for identification. In addition, it is important to understand that there is a vast difference between being able to define your different identities and having them defined for you. This interplay is noted in studies on the effects of teachers' and/or peers' racial and ethnic designation of ethnic minority students on the ways in which these students adapt to classroom and school culture (Connolly, 1998; Davidson, 1996, 1999; Erickson, 1987; Fergus, 2004; Fordham, 1988; Peshkin, 1991). In several studies, ethnic minority students project what is seemingly a "raceless" persona in order to escape the negative stigma associated with the racial/ethnic group signaled by their skin color (Fordham, 1988; Fordham & Ogbu, 1986). Therefore, what we can come to understand is that identity goes beyond situational or external forces, or individuals' choice or agency in layering their identification. Educators, particularly White educators, need to understand the power held in the boundary-making process of identification, which includes, "Who am I, who am I allowed to be, and what am I presumed to be?"

This process, of course, is couched within a larger societal framework of power relations that depends on the position of the individual (e.g., internal/external, in-group/out-group, White/non-White). These positionings dictate how such questions are answered.

When we are discussing the school context for Latino students, the racial/ethnic paradigm teachers are operating from functions as such a framework. Whether or not a White teacher acknowledges race/ethnicity and how the students construct their identification have monumental effects on the way students conceptualize their learning endeavor in the classroom. For instance, I've had several preservice teachers and veteran White teachers ask me whether they should allow students to use the N word; I ask them whether the culture of their classroom is about being a "Nigger"? And they usually respond no, which begs the question, "Then why do you allow them?" The real issue is not about the word but rather about the teacher who has opted to disengage from the construction of race and ethnicity in their classroom because he or she has not confronted his or her own interpretation of race/ethnicity.

## THE JOURNEY OF
## RACIAL AND CULTURAL COMPETENCE SKILL BUILDING

Unfortunately, within the process of racial/ethnic identification among Latinos, educators have situated themselves along language lines, mostly asking whether the students know English or Spanish. We typically have not acknowledged or situated the construction of a racial/ethnic identification for Latinos. The work of educators is not only to develop this knowledge base regarding Latinos but also to begin the journey of racial and cultural competence skill building. In the following section I provide some key skills that racially and culturally competent staff need.

## Skill #1: Confronting Racism: Opportunity to Learn (OTL) Moments

In the 1990s, while I was a student teacher, I was assigned to do my practicum at an all-White suburban school in Wisconsin. Although it was not the school where I had envisioned I would begin my education career, it became the schooling experience in which I enacted my racial and cultural competence. It was a challenge to teach in an all-White environment, much less to be the first person of color on the faculty in over 20 years. The cultural assaults began on the first day of "back to school" professional development in August. The keynote speaker, in commenting on the "diversity" of the staff, announced my presence to over 100 educators: "And we have a new faculty member . . . you look like a fly in a cup of milk." Although I experienced many of these moments of no cultural safety with the staff, the most profound and disturbing involved my White students. The reality of what my White students meant when they said, "Mr. Fergus, I'll bet you like Rodney King," or "I saw you in your ghetto mobile," or "Are you having a brotherly talk with the Black kids?" is actually a representation of their racialized world in a White middle-class community. And it is in such communities that employing OTL requires understanding when to engage without being worn out.

I'm often asked by superintendents and principals how they can recruit and retain more faculty of color. I always ask, "Can a person of color thrive in this community?" Often the answer is yes; however, it presumes that the liberalness that has allowed them to thrive as White people in the community is the type of liberalness that will permit people of color to thrive. Overall, the responsibility of being racially and culturally competent involves knowing when and how to confront the pervasive racist assaults that occur. For White teachers, the responsibility involves having to not only confront and acknowledge the privilege of their role, but also utilize their gate-keeping role to ensure equity.

Throughout my work with predominantly White suburban schools and districts, I inevitably end up talking to the few faculty of color they employ. Each one of them has similar stories of enduring racist behaviors from not only their colleagues but also White students. What they commonly convey is how debilitating it is to contend with cultural assaults and try to turn each event into an OTL. As one teacher of color said to me, "I'm just trying to survive." The racially and culturally competent White teachers and administrators need to own their role in addressing those OTL racist events.

## Skill #2: Creating Cultural Safety for Academic Success

Another element of being a racially and culturally competent White teacher is understanding your purpose in teaching all children, particularly children of color. An African American colleague in graduate school once told me and my wife, right before we had our first child: "Every year I would go to my child's teacher and say, "You can mess up their reading, I can fix that; you can mess up their math, I can fix that; but the day you start messing with their self-esteem I will be in your face." Such a perspective resonates with many parents of children of color. None of us wants to send our children into a school with predominantly White teachers who are unable to acknowledge their Whiteness and its implications in the schooling of children of color. Black and Latino parents want to know that their child will be culturally safe with White teachers. It is the responsibility of a racially and culturally competent White teacher to know the sociocultural significance of being a teacher to Black and Latino children; it is his or her job to arm these children with the resilience skills to survive racist assaults and find ways in which to thrive within such a reality.

The question becomes, What are the resilience skills that culturally safe classrooms should be providing? These skills include (but are not limited to) being able to acculturate to varying environments without assimilating, being able to unpack incidents of subtle and blatant racism, being able to understand White privilege and its purpose, and being able to celebrate culture, language, and race. Such skills must be nurtured by multiple adults involved in the development of children of color. Parents of children of color are constantly modeling the use of these skills; I think about my own kids whenever I get pulled over by the police, and I tell them to not say a word and to not make any sudden moves—they need to understand that our skin color is an affront to police. I teach them the skill of knowing when to call White people on their privileged behavior of cutting in front of people of color. I teach them the skill that sometimes their White teachers will reprimand them for behavior their White peers are permitted to get away with in the classroom. I teach them to not let White people ask to touch their hair simply because they've never felt curly hair. Finally, I teach them that although White privilege operates as cultural behavior inherent in structural processes, we never know which White person is on a quest to remove such behaviors. Thus, it is these resilience skills that students of color need to develop in a culturally safe environment, an environment that understands the significant impact of racism on the mental health of people of color. In order to construct this mental health space, teachers need to know why these resilience skills are relevant in the lives of these children.

## CONCLUSION

The construction of racial and cultural competence is a complicated notion that must entail an understanding of how variation exists within many racial and ethnic groups. My discussion about racial/ethnic identification and its complexity in relation to Latinos is intended to situate identification as a key priority of educators with racial and cultural competence. Many educators find themselves in the midst of a field in which the practice of teaching is centered on the learning gap that children of color maintain. And in this endeavor we have omitted the significance of the conditions for learning, which involve more than the number of classroom libraries or the type of balanced literacy that will affect standardized scores. We have abandoned a focus on the standardized skills teachers need to have in order to be effective in classrooms with optimal learning conditions. In sum, as we continue into the 21st century and the population of Latinos grows to assume the position of the largest minority group, the challenge becomes training teachers to own the notion of being racially and culturally competent as a tool for their academic endeavor.

## REFERENCES

Barth, F. (1969). *Ethnic groups and boundaries: The social organization of culture difference.* Boston: Little, Brown.

Bashi, V. (1998). Racial categories matter because racial hierarchies matter: A commentary. *Ethnic and Racial Studies, 21,* 959–968.

Cornell, S. (1988). *The return of the native: American Indian political resurgence.* New York: Oxford University Press.

Cornell, S. (1996). The variable ties that bind: Content and circumstance in ethnic processes. *Ethnic and Racial Studies, 19*, 266–289.

Davidson, A. L. (1996). *Making and molding identity in schools: Student narratives on race, gender, and academic engagement.* Albany: State University of New York Press.

Davidson, A. L. (1999). Negotiating social differences. *Urban Education, 34*, 338–369.

Erickson, E. D. (1987). Transformation and school success: The politics and culture of educational achievement. *Anthropology and Education Quarterly, 18*(4), 335–356.

Espino, R., & Franz, M. (2002). Latino phenotypic discrimination revisited: The impact of skin color on occupational status. *Social Science Quarterly, 83*, 612–623.

Fergus, E. (2002). *Everyone sees my skin color differently: Phenotype and ethnic identification in the perceptions of opportunity and academic orientation of Mexican and Puerto Rican Youth.* Unpublished dissertation.

Fergus, E. (2004). *Skin color and identity formation: Perceptions of opportunity and academic orientation among Puerto Rican and Mexican youth.* New York: Routledge.

Fordham, S. (1988). Racelessness as a factor in Black students' school success: Pragmatic strategy or pyrrhic victory? *Harvard Educational Review, 58*(1), 54–84.

Fordham, S., & Ogbu, J. (1986). Black students' school success: Coping with the burden of acting White. *Urban Review, 18*(3), 176–206.

Glazer, N., & Moynihan, D. (1970). *Beyond the melting pot.* Cambridge.: MIT Press.

Gordon, M. (1961). Assimilation in America: Theory and reality. *DAEDALUS: Journal of the American Academy of Arts and Sciences, 90*(2), 263–285.

Hall, S. (1990). Cultural identity and diaspora. In J. Rutherford (Ed.), *Identity: Community, culture, difference* (pp. 222–237). London: Lawrence & Wishart.

Hochschild, J., Burch, T., & Weaver, V. (2005). *Effects of skin color bias in SES on political activities and attitudes.* Unpublished manuscript.

Logan, J. (2003). *How race counts for Hispanic Americans.* Unpublished manuscript, State University of New York at Albany, Mumford Center.

Nagel, J. (1986). The political construction of ethnicity. In S. Olzak & J. Nagel (Eds.), *Competitive ethnic relations* (pp. 69–90). New York: Academic Press.

Nagel, J. (1994). Constructing ethnicity: Creating and recreating ethnic identity and culture. *Social Problems, 41*, 152–176.

Omi, M., & Winant, H. (1994). *Racial formation in the United States: From the 1960s to the 1990s.* New York: Routledge.

Padilla, F. (1985). *Latino ethnic consciousness.* Notre Dame, IN: University of Notre Dame Press.

Patterson, O. (1975). Context and choice in ethnic allegiance: A theoretical framework and Caribbean case study. In N. Glazer & D. Moynihan (Eds.), *Ethnicity: Theory and experiences* (pp. 304–349). Cambridge, MA: Harvard University Press.

Peshkin, A. (1991). *The color of strangers, the color of friends: The play of ethnicity in school and community.* Chicago: University of Chicago Press.

Portes, A., & MacLeod, D. (1996).What shall I call myself? Hispanic identity formation in the second generation. *Ethnic and Racial Studies, 19*(3), 523–547.

Saenz, R., & Aguirre, B. (1991). The dynamics of Mexican ethnic identity. *Ethnic Groups, 9*(1), 17–32.

Yancey, W., Ericksen, E., & Richard, J. (1976). Emergent ethnicity: A review and reformulation. *American Sociological Review, 41*, 391–403.

# CHAPTER FOUR

# Storytelling About Racial and Cultural Competence with a Focus on Multiculturalism

*Carl A. Grant*

## STORY GENRES ABOUT THE EDUCATION OF STUDENTS OF COLOR

There is a rich but still too often unexplored series of resources about the education of students of color. Among these resources are several genres.

One genre focuses on stories about the legal battles that have been fought over such issues as the elimination of de jure segregation and parental advocacy of the right to have their children taught in their native language. Stories in this genre include the struggles involving the many people who helped bring about the end of de jure segregation by their participation in the legal battles that resulted in the U.S. Supreme Court's 1954 decision in *Brown v. Board of Education*. Other stories tell of the activism of the members of the Chinese American community who demanded that Chinese American children with limited English proficiency receive instruction in schools in their native language. This activism led to the U.S. Supreme Court's 1974 decision in *Lau v. Nichols*, which ruled in favor of the students.

Another genre focuses on efforts to inform society about the mis-education of students of color, as well as efforts to change the pedagogy used to educate students of color. The storylines in this genre tell of how students of color have been mis-educated (e.g., Woodson, 1933/1990); how students of color have had their language and culture stolen (e.g., Adams, 1995); how students of color faced day-to-day injustices during school desegregation (e.g., Bridges, 1999); and how students of color have been ostracized and resegregated in so-called desegregated schools (e.g., Orfield & Eaton, 1997).

Still another genre tells of the struggle to make the schooling and the education of students of color successful. The stories within this genre tell of people, but not only school people, who worked to make schooling and the education of students of color successful through their explanation of how the life of people of color is situated in an unfair and unjust society. These stories include narratives such as *The Souls of Black Folk* by W. E. B. DuBois, *Pedagogy of the Oppressed* by Paulo Freire, and *Strangers from a Different Shore* by Ronald Takaki. These stories, as well as countless others—and let me emphasize *countless others*—inform some, but not enough, of the ideas that educators and others employ today when they work to educate students of color successfully and provide all students with a multicultural and social justice education (e.g., the struggle of people of color to locate their identity and find their place in a dominant society; a liberating pedagogy that enables and empowers the common person to act upon and transform his or her world; the trials and tribulations of new immigrants as they arrive and make their way in society; and the triple oppression of women of color).

My point is that much of what I presently strive to do to enhance the racial and cultural competence of relatively new, as well as veteran, practicing teachers and teacher educators is built upon the groundwork created by others. So the story—*my story* (and probably your story)—that tells of my experiences, current thinking, and suggestions to practicing teachers and teacher educators is greatly influenced by the work of many others. I borrow from the old but wise expression, "We stand on the shoulders of others." However, as I acknowledge where I stand, I also am arguing that there are excellent ideas and resources still being developed for teaching students of color in a manner that seeks to ensure that they have socially and economically flourishing lives.

Now, adhering to the advice and direction of the editors, my chapter continues as follows: First, I address the source and context of my (recent) experiences that influence my thoughts and issues about multiculturalism and racial and cultural competence in a section I call "Through the Eyes of My Grandchildren." Second, I elaborate on my current thinking about multiculturalism and racial and cultural competence. Finally, I offer suggestions for educators to become racially and culturally competent. However, before I continue, I should acknowledge that the State of Ohio writing team's definition of "cultural competence," which serves as one of the foundational pillars for this volume, expresses very well the ideas and actions of many who work to bring multiculturalism to schools, culturally relevant pedagogy to classrooms, and social justice to society. The definition was:

> Culturally competent teachers see differences among students as assets. They create caring learning communities where individuals and cultural heritages, including languages, are expressed and valued. They use cultural and individual knowledge about their students, their families, and their communities to design instructional strategies that build upon and link home and school experiences. They challenge stereotypes and intolerance. They serve as change agents by thinking and acting critically to address inequities distinguished by (but not limited to) race, language, culture, socioeconomics, family structures, and gender. Beyond using images, literature, and other forms of expression that represent students' diverse cultures and backgrounds, teachers understand, affirm, and use students' home and primary languages, communication styles, and family structure for learning and discipline.

## THROUGH THE EYES OF MY GRANDCHILDREN

> Color is not a human or personal reality; it is a political reality.
> —James Baldwin, 1985, p. 379

My thoughts about issues of racial and cultural competence are greatly informed by what I learn from the literature, and by my work with students and faculty from diverse racial, gender, religious, sexuality, and (dis)ability groups at the pre-K–12 and higher education levels. However, over the past 11 years, my collective experiences—my critical memory—also have informed me as an active participant in the growth, education, and development of my two grandchildren, Gavin, age 11, and Amaya, age 5. Observations of their in- and out-of-school life experiences and activities inform my understanding of the racism that they and other pre-K–12 students of color endure and how

White privilege is ever present. From my observations, I see that *isms* are everywhere, even in the lives of preteens. True, most of the *isms* are not operating at the individual and institutional level in society as strongly and as blatantly as they were 50 or 60 years ago. Nevertheless, although somewhat more nuanced, the *isms* still wreak almost as much oppression and evil as they always have.

Story after story is told about the African American male students who are placed or nearly placed in special education classes and how such placements affect their lives (Lamothe, 2007). It is unusual to be around a group of African American parents and not have someone in the group tell a story about "special education" and their daughter or son; in most cases, the story is about a Black boy. I, too, have a story; it's about my grandson, Gavin. The story highlights how I see, or in this case don't see, multiculturalism or racial and cultural competence operating in a setting that is multiracial and multicultural.

The school he was attending informed Gavin's mother, my daughter Alicia, that it wanted to "test" him. Gavin, a 3rd grader at the time, was reported to get off task and not to completely comply with school rules. He would not stay seated in the same way that most (and my use of the word *most* is significant) of the other students would stay in their seats. When Gavin's mother was sent the parental consent form to sign in order to test Gavin, I suggested that she junk the idea. I argued, based on my teaching experience and on having done academic work (more than homework) with Gavin almost every night during the school year and during the summer, that there was nothing wrong with him. He did not have a learning problem, and not staying confined to his seat should not make him a candidate for special education.

Nevertheless, Alicia wore me down, arguing, "Dad, can you say with absolute certainty that there is nothing wrong with Gavin? And, if there is, we need to know sooner rather than later, so we can take action. We should not take a chance." To complicate this story, it was only a few weeks before summer vacation when the consent form arrived, and Alicia was informed that the testing would not take place until the new school year. Thus, Alicia would have to wait, worry, and wonder all summer whether her son had a problem.

At her request, the school gave Alicia information about a private psychologist who was school-approved and who therefore could perform the test. An appointment was scheduled with the private psychologist, and Gavin was tested.

After the tests had been administered and evaluated, the psychologist asked why Gavin was being tested and who had suggested that he should be tested. When told the story of the school's reason for having Gavin tested, he said we should tell the school (show them the test results) that there was nothing wrong with Gavin. He saw nothing in the test results that would make Gavin a candidate for special education. He went on to say that Gavin was a typical 9-year-old boy. He did, however, suggest some strategies that we could use that would help Gavin in school, so Alicia did come away with "something."

All throughout this experience, I contended that if Gavin were White, he would have been seen as a typical boy, and the disciplinary system of the school and the practices of labeling and categorizing that construct Black boys as individuals with behavior problems would not have been put into motion. I am reminded of what Ann Ferguson argues in Chapter 3, "School Rules," of her book, *Bad Boys: Public Schools in the Making of Black Masculinity* (2001). She writes:

> School rules govern and regulate children's bodily, linguistic, and emotional expression. They are an essential element of sorting and ranking technologies of an educational system that is organized around the search for an establishment of a ranked difference among children. (p. 50)

Gavin's story informs us that cultural sensitivity, which the National Maternal and Child Health Resource Center on Cultural Competency (1997) defines as "knowing that cultural differences as well as similarities exist, without assigning values, i.e., better or worse, right or wrong, to those cultural differences" (p. 10), is understood and acted upon, at best, in a superficial manner in too many classrooms and schools. In addition, cultural competence, defined by Cross, Bazron, Dennis, and Isaacs (1989) as "a set of congruent behaviors, attitudes, and policies that come together in a system, agency, or among professionals and enables that system, agency, or those professionals to work effectively in cross cultural situations" (p. 1), is not operating in a significant way for many African American male students.

Finally, before I put this story to rest, my concern is with the other Gavins of the world, the ones whose families cannot afford to pay over $1,000 for their child to be tested. Many parents would be left with the headache of dealing with the issue over the summer and having their child wondering, "Is something wrong with me?" and/or "Why me? Because what I did was no different than what some of my White classmates were doing." Students' voices, whether those of my grand-children or some other children, are informative about whether or not racial and cultural competence exists in schools. Students, if we listen to them, can alert us to the racial and cultural competencies that educators should develop.

## MY CURRENT THINKING ABOUT MULTICULTURALISM AND RACIAL AND CULTURAL COMPETENCE

Much of my current thinking about racial and cultural competence is influenced by both national events such as Hurricane Katrina and international trends such as globalization, along with my ongoing research about multiculturalism. Before I proceed, I would like to give the definition of multiculturalism that is guiding my thinking, because there are several other definitions that are used in the education literature. Multiculturalism is a concerted plan (i.e., strategy) that employs extensive knowledge of people, histories, and contexts in an effort to challenge the current state of politics, socioeconomic status, race, gender, (dis)ability, and sexual orientation status quo.

In addition, the definition by Banks and Banks (1993) is useful: "Multiculturalism is a philosophical position and movement that assumes that gender, ethnic, racial, and cultural diversity of a pluralistic society should be reflected in all of its institutionalized structures" (p. 7). Furthermore, multicultural education contends that a power relation exists between people and groups, and, since power is sometimes elusive and difficult to identify and articulate, movement toward multiculturalism without recognizing and mapping power within a particular environment most likely will meet with resistance and failure.

### Hurricane Katrina and Multiculturalism

The reaction to Hurricane Katrina by the civil authorities and the media showed a blatant form of racism, including a racialized discourse. It was *anti-multiculturalism* and *racial and cultural incompetence* in perhaps every way imaginable. Their reaction was a return to the days of Jim Crow: benign neglect, and separate and unequal, all rolled up into one. The one small ray of light (let me call it a small ray of multicultural light) was that Hurricane Katrina forced all Americans to witness or become participant observers in the racism which is still too often denied to exist in U.S. society (e.g., Grant, 2006).

Not since the 1960s, during the Civil Rights Movement, could one watch on television the horrific treatment in the United States of so many African Americans. During the Civil Rights Movement, it was snarling dogs, water from high-pressure fire hoses, and White police officials swinging billy clubs that were the tools used to inflict pain on African Americans and other civil rights workers. During the first decade of the 21st century, the tools that inflicted pain on the African Americans who were victims of Katrina were arguably more severe; they were the tools of denial and disregard: denial of the basic sources of life, including food, shelter, and water, and disregard that some African Americans died horrible and unnecessary deaths, often alone.

The racialized discourse I speak of was the media reporting of Hurricane Katrina. Watching television, it was immediately and painfully obvious to me and many other African Americans that race was a key factor in the government response to the people stranded in New Orleans, most of whom were Black (Thomma, 2005). The media was slow to report on racism as a major contributing factor to the lack of an immediate rescue of African Americans who were floating, wading in the water, and standing on rooftops. The discourse in the media was one of benign neglect, or dysconscious racism (King, 1991). In addition, it often has been pointed out that institutional racism is alive and well in the media (McGowan, 2002). A fair question to ponder is, "If there were more reporters of color, and the management staffs of the various media outlets had received a multicultural education, would they have been so dis-conscious about what was taking place before their very eyes?"

What television and newspapers first reported was that Blacks were looting and robbing. Racism became a part of the media discourse only when race could not be ignored or mentally pushed away as the television pictures showed the horrible conditions African Americans were facing. More than a year later, as I write this chapter, concerns about New Orleans and Hurricane Katrina are sometimes in the news as the hurricane season approaches, but discussions of the systemic racism and the absence of multiculturalism or racial and cultural competence have almost disappeared from the public discourse.

## Globalization and Multiculturalism

Globalization is everywhere. It has caused Thomas L. Friedman to argue that because of globalization and technology, *The World Is Flat.* Friedman (2006) argues that:

> Globalization is the newfound power for individuals to collaborate and compete globally. And the phenomenon that is enabling, empowering, and enjoining individuals and small groups to go global so easily and so seamlessly is what I call the *flat-world platform.* The flat-world platform is the product of a convergence of the personal computer (which allowed every individual to become the author of his or her own content in digital form) with fiber-optic cable (which suddenly allowed all those individuals to access more and more digital content around the world for next to nothing) with the rise of work flow software (which enables individuals all over the world to collaborate on that same digital content from anywhere, regardless of the distances between them). (pp. 10–11)

Whereas the influences of globalization were becoming clear to some before 1983, they became crystal clear to all, especially educators, in 1983 with the publication of *A Nation at Risk: The Imperative for Educational Reform* by the National Commission on Excellence in Education. The Commission declared:

> If an unfriendly foreign power had attempted to impose on America the mediocre educational performance that exists today, we might well have viewed it as an act of war. As it stands, we have allowed this to happen to ourselves. We have even squandered the gains in student achievement made in the wake of the Sputnik challenge. Moreover, we have dismantled essential support systems which help to make those gains possible. We have, in effect, committed an act of unthinking unilateral education disarmament. (p. 5)

Although I say the discussions of globalization are everywhere, what I have not addressed is the quality of these discussions. By this I mean much of the content of these discussions is about four aspects of globalization: trade, capital movement, movement of people, and the spread of knowledge (and technology). What is absent in this discussion is any serious attention to education. Discussions of education/schooling and globalization tend to focus on: (1) how to prepare a workforce to function in our technological society; (2) whether education should help engender a new "humanism"; and (3) how education/schooling lags behind the "world outside of school."

The first discussion comes out of a discourse that is concerned with how globalization is influencing education and, in return, how education/schooling can influence globalization. Wells and colleagues (1998) support this position when they argue that globalization will

> mean a more competitive and deregulated educational system modeled after a free market but with more pressure on it to assure that the next generation of workers are prepared for some amorphous job market of the 21st century. It will also mean that educational systems will increasingly provide the sites of struggle over the meaning and power of national identity and a national culture. And finally, schools will no doubt also be the sites of various counter-hegemonic movements and pedagogies. (quoted in Azad, 2004, p. 5)

Finally, on this point, Azad argues that:

> An important component of globalization in relation to education is the need for producing higher quality manpower that can successfully face competition in the world markets. This would imply selecting the best possible human material and giving them education of highest quality. (p. 9)

The second discussion is characterized in the Delors Commission (1996) report, which argued that

> Education should help engender a new humanism that contains an essential ethical component and sets considerable store by knowledge of, and respect for, the culture and spiritual values of different civilizations, as much needed counter weight to a globalization that would otherwise be seen only in economical or technological terms. (p. 7)

The third discussion is about how schools lag behind the "real world." This point was obvious in the statement I quoted above from *A Nation at Risk*.

Neubauer (2007), and many others, tell us that this remains pretty much the same as it was decades ago. Instruction is highly structured, ability grouping and segregation by age remain firmly in place, and textbooks hold sway to what is taught and how it is taught. In other words, "One could argue that we are continuing to organize education to train and educate people to work and succeed in a world that increasingly no longer exists" (Neubauer, 2007, p. 311).

The purpose and meaning of education in these points ignores Thomas Jefferson's idea that we need an informed citizenry. The discussions about education avoid or disregard critiques, both analytical and civic. Instead, the discussions that we do see in relation to education are ones that address international comparisons of achievement test scores.

Such ideas demand a multicultural education that teaches students the 3Rs, but also teaches the tools of analysis that will help students to investigate/interrogate the effects of globalization on the global climate and on those who are poor and live in nonindustrialized countries. In addition, multicultural education should inform students that the educational system increasingly is being forced into a market model and increasingly is moving away from the traditional concept of education as a public social good with attention toward the "whole" individual.

## SUGGESTIONS FOR BECOMING RACIALLY AND CULTURALLY COMPETENT EDUCATORS

Maureen Gillette and I, in *Learning to Teach Everyone's Children: Equity, Empowerment, and Education That Is Multicultural* (2007), identify and address ten things that teacher candidates can do to become racially and culturally competent. Space does not allow me to completely repeat the ten in full. However, I will give the first line from each point, and add one more point.

- Get experience with all types of learners and their families.
- Get political.
- Take your education seriously.
- Become aware that you are a role model and act accordingly.
- Become active in your school community.
- Volunteer in or join organizations or get involved with a group that comprises people who are different from you.
- Develop ways to "recharge your battery."
- Practice democratic principles.
- Learn to identify allies.
- Study effective teachers.

Finally, teacher candidates have perhaps—unknown or little known to them—a personal, almost selfish reason to become racially and culturally competent educators. Teaching from a multicultural education perspective may prevent them from wanting to leave teaching after 1 or 2 years or becoming dissatisfied with the profession, as is the case with so many of their peers. Teaching from this perspective, and becoming racially and culturally competent, will make their instruction much more intellectual, culturally engaging, and academically enriching, and it will help them to understand the real reason why learning is dynamic and why both students and teachers must be life-long learners.

## REFERENCES

Adams, D. W. (1995). *Education for extinction: American Indians and the boarding school experience, 1875–1928*. Lawrence: University Press of Kansas.

Azad, J. L. (2004). Globalization and its impact on education: A challenge and an opportunity. Available at http:/72.14205.104/search?q=cache: aB9jvkyOJ:cie.du.ac.in?Globalization%2

Baldwin, J. (1985). *The price of the ticket*. New York: St. Martin's.

Banks, J., & Banks, C. A. (Eds.) (1993). *Multicultural education: Issues and perspectives* (2nd ed.). Boston: Allyn & Bacon.

Bridges, R. (1999). *Through my eyes*. New York: Scholastic

Cross, T., Bazron, B., Dennis K., & Isaacs, M. (1989). *Toward a culturally competent system of care* (Vol. 1). Washington, DC: Georgetown University.

Delors, J., et al. (1996). *Learning, the treasure within: Report to UNESCO of the International Commission on Education for the Twenty-first Century*. Paris: UNESCO.

Dubois, W.E. B. (1993). *The souls of black folk*. New York: Knopf. (Original work published 1903)

Ferguson, A. A. (2001). *Bad boys: Public schools in the making of black masculinity*. Ann Arbor: University of Michigan Press.

Freidman, T. (2006). *The world is flat: A brief history of the twenty-first century*. New York: Farrar, Straus & Giroux.

Freire, P. (2000). *Pedagogy of the oppressed*. New York: Continuum. (Original work published 1970)

Grant, C. A. (2006). Multiculturalism, race, and the public interest: Hanging on to great-great-granddaddy's legacy. In G. Ladson-Billings & W. F. Tate (Eds.), *Education research in the public interest: Social justice, action, and policy* (pp. 158–172). New York: Teachers College Press.

Grant, C. A., & Gillette, M. (2007). *Learning to teach everyone's children: Equity, empowerment, and education that is multicultural*. Belmont, CA: Thomson & Wadsworth.

King, J. E. (1991). Dysconscious racism: Ideology, identity, and the miseducation of teachers. *Journal of Negro Education, 60*(2), 133–146.

Lamothe, E., Jr. (2007, May 3). More blacks land in special education. News-Gazette.com. Available at http://www.news-gazette.com/special/achievegap/index.cfm?page=story&id=9

McGowan, W. (2002). *Coloring the news: How political correctness has corrupted American journalism.* San Francisco: Encounter Books.

National Commission on Excellence in Education. (1983). *A nation at risk: The imperative for educational reform*: Washington, DC: U.S. Government Printing Office.

National Maternal and Child Health Resource Center on Cultural Competency. (1997). *Journey towards cultural competency: Lessons learned.* Austin, TX: Author.

Neubauer, D. (2007, July). Globalization, interdependence and education. *Frontiers of Education in China, 2*(3), 309–324.

Orfield, G., & Eaton, S. E. (1996). *Dismantling desegregation: The quiet reversal of* Brown vs. Board of Education. New York: New Press.

Takaki, R. (1989). *Strangers from a different shore.* Boston: Little Brown

Thomma, E. (2005, September). How Bush blew it. *Newsweek,* pp. 30–38.

Wells, S. A., Sibyll, C., Slayton, J., Allen, R. L., & Vasudeva, A. (1998). Globalization and educational change. In A. Hargreaves (Ed.), *Extending educational change: International handbook of educational change* (vol. 5, pp. 322–348). London: Kluwer Academic.

Woodson, C. (1990). *Mis-education of the Negro.* Trenton, NJ: Africa World Press. (Original work published 1933)

# CHAPTER FIVE

# How Best to Develop Preservice Teachers' Racial and Cultural Competence: Reflections on Pedagogy and Practice in the University Classroom

*Jennifer E. Obidah*

## A CAPSULE JOURNEY OF LIVING WITH RACISM

I was not born in America, but my child was. I have dual citizenship as an American and a Barbadian. Most of my life thus far has been lived in the United States, although I was born in Barbados, a small Caribbean island. I immigrated to Brooklyn, New York, with my brother to live with my mother. She had come a year earlier to live with my father, who had been living in Brooklyn for several years.

Because of my family's economic situation, I went to work first before I could even contemplate pursuing education. In many ways I lived two lives. I perceived myself as being exposed to White America through my baby-sitting job, and I lived in Black America in the evenings and on the weekends. I was unimpressed with the life of White America that I saw through my job. I took care of two wonderful kids in a house located on a very quiet, tree-lined street in Queens. My employees were a young couple, both doctors (at the time they were completing their residencies) with two young kids they hardly spent time with because of their work schedules. Sometimes when they were both on call, I would spend the night with the children, but the quietness of that neighborhood always made me long to go home to the liveliness and energy of my Brooklyn neighborhood. As I described in an earlier work (Obidah & Teel, 2001), I enjoyed both the good and bad of my life in Bed-Stuy. I didn't think of my neighborhood as a place to "get out" of. It was home.

Life in my old neighborhood was not, nor will it ever be, one-dimensional. My friends and I did not refer to ourselves as at-risk, impoverished, disadvantaged, or any of the other negatively tinged descriptions in the education literature I read during my years of graduate school. We had full lives despite the circumstances of living in our part of town. In some ways we were at risk, since many of my friends went in directions that did not enhance the quality of their adult lives. Yet, I think that it is important for teachers, especially, not to perceive kids' potential to succeed academically only through their limited economic circumstances. Such teachers might miss the inner potential of some kids, like me, who, with a little luck and determination, coupled with guidance and support from the adults in their lives, choose the path of higher education. In other words, there are elements of our students that the economic exteriors of their lives cannot tell us. We can know what's in their hearts only if they trust us enough to show us. My adolescent memories still act as a constant reminder that people not only survive in economically disadvantaged neighborhoods, but they live as well.

My early years of living and working in New York City were when and where I learned about racism. I learned about racism when I was treated as a potential thief rather than a potential shopper in department stores in New York City; when it became clear that there were places in the city where I was expected to work but never live; when White teachers (in high school) and professors (in college and university) expected from me academic failure rather than academic success. I became angry living with racism, and I confronted its many manifestations. Yet, confronting racism made only my anger obvious, not the racist acts. This is why I concluded that racism in American society is endemic as a ghost, an illusion.

Pertaining to people's actions, Berlak, in Chapter 2 of this volume, discusses people's racist behavior as operating for the most part from their "adaptive unconscious," which is maintained by American society's ideological commitment to White supremacy. The notion of people's adaptive unconscious provided me with another theoretical lens through which to reflect on the illusionist aspect of racist acts. Through my lived experiences, I came to believe that racist acts often were not "seen" by the perpetrator without a witness who corroborated the victim's view that such an act took place. If there is no witness, then proving that an act occurred is often impossible. On the wings of inflicted pain, the victim is transported to the land of surrealism: Did that really happen? Did he just say that? Did she just do that? Was it me? Maybe I misread what happened. Finally, hopefully, before anger is internalized and damages one's self-esteem, if one continues to overtly struggle against oppression and acts of injustice, the second-guessing of self lessens and the "self" as a witness is empowered.

However, one becomes angry before one becomes free. Thus far, anger is one of the most powerful emotions I've seen that, initially, fuels the oppressed from a position of victim to a position of empowered freedom. But holding on to the anger after the transition to freedom also can lead to self-destruction. I'm grateful to role models like Nelson Mandela who provide an example of what it means to live free in the aftermath of racial injustices. He models a path to freedom that releases the need for anger in this way, and such a life is one I constantly try to emulate.

I taught my first university education course in 1990. In all, I've taught at four universities in three states. Along the way, people's questioning of my ability to effectively address the issues of race and racism in the course of building preservice teachers' racial and cultural competencies has emanated in various forms. Early on, I had both students and colleagues question my "youthfulness" and its potential detriment to my ability to impart knowledge.

Later on, I had students become angry because I "talked about race all the time!" In my courses, I've had White students be bold enough to tell me that they threw our co-authored book (Obidah & Teel, 2001) across the room because I took advantage of Karen. I've also had African American students rightly confront me about teaching only to the White students in the class because race and racism were addressed primarily as issues of which the White students should become more aware.

On only one occasion, I had African American colleagues question me about whether I was qualified to address these topics, since I wasn't born in America. However, for the most part, I've been questioned by my White colleagues. I've had colleagues who wondered out loud about the place of emotion in academic settings; whether my courses were too "touchy-feely"; and whether I could get tenure based on my focus on the implementation of practical solutions through which these issues can be addressed in K–12 classrooms.

Through all of these experiences, I've honed my knowledge base—reading scholars more adept at elucidating their perspectives on race and racism. These scholars had more years of grappling theoretically with the issues that inform my passion as an educator. I've also honed my pedagogy and teaching craft by constantly examining my practices, seeking help and learning from fellow educators and my students.

Every experience discussed above has taught me more about how race and racism and White privilege operate in American society and, in particular, in educational systems. These experiences deeply informed who I am as a teacher educator and what I bring to my university classroom. The above paragraphs also serve as a capsule of my journey with racism. Reflecting on my identity, the influence of racism, and the ways I've chosen along the way to actively address the negative influences of racism in my life, make me confident as a teacher educator, facilitating preservice teachers' learning about their identity and the influence of racism in their lives.

## PREPARING TEACHERS TO BE
## RACIALLY AND CULTURALLY COMPETENT

In this section I focus on my journey of developing preservice teachers' racial and cultural competencies. This development occurs through my teaching students about the elusive elements of racism and how these elements are embedded in their fears and concerns about their future students and about teaching in urban schools in general. To detail this process, I analyze students' journal entries that resulted from class readings and the accompanying activities used in class to bring to life perspectives detailed in the readings. Additionally, I analyze my teaching practices in these classes, comparing what I taught and responded to with how, in reflection, I would now respond. Lastly, I discuss emerging issues and detail any lessons I've learned from analyzing students' writings in similar courses over the years, in particular those from the course I focus on in this chapter. Through these reflections, I hope to respond to the task of suggesting how preservice and veteran teachers can better prepare themselves to deal with the self-realizations that occur as they continue their journey of becoming racially and culturally competent educators.

The quotes in this chapter come from the students who took my course titled "Cultural Identity" in the fall of 2002. Thirteen instructors collaboratively developed the course over the summer prior to when the course was taught. The course took place weekly for 2 hours, and themes were covered over two classes. The roll in my section of the class comprised 16 students, although the entire cohort of students working on their master's in teaching degree took the course at the same time, covering the same syllabus, but was divided into a number of sections.

## Course Activities

Five themes were covered in the course: identity, culture, positionality, oppression, and allies. Due to page limits, all of the activities that accompanied these themes cannot be discussed in this chapter. I will briefly describe the activities my students and I participated in that I will refer to in this chapter. These activities are the construction of an "I Am From" poem; the Forced Corners activity; the A/B Line; and the Power Scatter.

*"I Am From" Poem.* This poem, written by George Ella Lyon, was adopted by Linda Christensen, whose article informs teacher educators how to use this poem as an activity in their classes. This activity affirms students' identity in relation to family, neighborhoods, culture, and heritage, and encourages teachers to make students feel "significant" in their classrooms.

*Forced Corners.* In this activity students are "forced" to move to the four corners of the classroom and discuss or stand quietly beneath the topic listed there. The topics were gender, sexuality/sexual orientation, race/ethnicity, and spirituality/religion. Once in the corner, students were instructed to either discuss the topic or just stand and look around quietly to see to which corner their classmates were "forced" to go.

*A/B Line.* This activity is designed to assist students in unveiling social status and to take a closer look at where their identity places them in the societal hierarchy. Participants are asked to line up in two straight lines facing each other. The "A line" represents status, prestige, privilege, and power, and the "B line" represents oppression, discrimination, and disadvantage. Throughout the activity each participant moves to the line that best represents his or her status in relation to the prompt read aloud.

*Power Scatter.* This activity begins with students lining up in straight lines holding hands. As prompts are put to the students, they are told, "If this applies to you, take two steps forward and if it does not, take two steps back." Students also are told to hold hands until they can't hold on anymore. This exercise physically demonstrates that as a result of one's group affiliation, coupled with individual experiences, some people are at the privileged front of society and others are at a disadvantage.

As an educator in this program, I relished the program's overt preparation of students to face the difficult issues of teaching in the urban inner-city classroom. In particular, having students process the fact that the majority of them come from different racial, cultural, and class backgrounds than their future students was a task I eagerly took on. My eagerness came in part from personal conviction, but also, in this program, from being encouraged by colleagues and the teaching environment. I enjoyed teaching in the ally-filled environment that we sought to create. This support system made what I knew from past experience to be a difficult journey—often for students and sometimes for myself—seem less emotionally taxing, especially since I did not have to worry about my colleagues questioning the appropriateness or validity of the course.

Using carefully chosen texts, accompanied by activities that brought the issues discussed in the texts to light, I introduced students to concepts such as oppression, racism, and White privilege. For some of my students, particularly many of the European and Asian American students, these were very new concepts about which to dialogue, particularly in a mixed-race group. In the remainder of the chapter, I write about the processes students went through mentally and emotionally to grasp these concepts over the course of a 10-week quarter, and how these reflections continue to inform my pedagogy. All students' names are pseudonyms.

Acknowledging that the journey would be a difficult one, the course was structured to first allow students moments of self-affirmation: who they perceived themselves to be at the start of their journey. We accomplished this by writing "I Am From" poems. Below are excerpts from some of the students' poems.

> *Eileen*: I'm from Kentucky Derby; the 1986 University of
> Louisville NCAA basketball champions; ballet, tap, and jazz
> class with Lola Roberts; Haydn and Mozart piano pieces.

*Lisa*: I'm from rodeos, Camp Fire Girls, and Rawhide Ranch where I spent many summers.

*Shauna*: I'm from Indian fry bread, "Yutaheh" and late-night Pow-wows.

*Fanisha*: I'm from gumbo, greens, cornbread, and other southern foods that my family enjoys.

*Emily*: I'm from a family who does not encourage me to ask questions because its "ma-fan"! (too much trouble). [class discussions 10/1/02]

Students sharing their "I Am From" poems created very powerful moments of classroom interactions. Interestingly, because they were all in the same age cohort, the same music (Michael Jackson and Paula Abdul) and favorite toys (Cabbage Patch dolls) were repeated in poems across race and class. Afterward, students were asked to write journal reflections on constructing their own poems as well as listening to the poems written by classmates, and many of them remarked on these similarities.

## Concepts Covered

The poem activity allowed students glimpses into their peers' lives—albeit heavily edited versions—but even such glimpses allowed students to see how different or similar their lives were from one another. Finding common issues through which to bond was an important benefit of the exercise, since, in the weeks following, differences—between one another and between them and their future students—were emphasized. The emphasis resulted from students' introduction to concepts such as oppression, privilege, and racism.

*Oppression.* Young (2000) describes contemporary oppression as "systemic restraints embedded in unquestioned norms, habits, symbols, in the assumptions underlying institutional rules and the collective consequence of following those rules" (p. 36). This article was helpful to students because it gave a new and contrasting meaning to what they perceived as oppression. For example, Lisa, a White female student, wrote:

I equate [physical] suffering with oppression so I don't use the term to describe the state of oppression in America [and] I haven't been able to see the suffering/oppression that minorities go through everyday here in America. [JN 11/12/02]

To Lisa, the type of overt human suffering she equated with active oppression was not apparent in American society. Thus, it was difficult for her to understand how minorities in America could be oppressed today (as opposed to the historical oppression of enslavement). Reading Young's text, as well as other students' writings shared in class, afforded Lisa other perspectives. Shauna, another White student who, interestingly, for part of her life was raised on an Indian reservation, wrote:

> When one looks at "the oppressor" it is necessary to go beyond the individual to see what systematic influences are shaping the individual's actions. How do the media portray people of color? How does this [portrayal] influence the way in which people form stereotypes? How do laws enable segregation? These and many other questions need to be evaluated when considering the sources of oppression. [JN 11/12/02]

Shauna had grappled with issues of oppression before taking the course. As she wrote in her journal, her experiences with these issues began in her undergraduate years. It was then that she was forced to deal with the assumptions of a "White" identity that she felt was assigned to her in college. She had not hitherto identified with this aspect of her identity, mainly because of her life experience of spending many cherished childhood moments on an Indian reservation with her mother's family. Her perspective, when shared in class, was very helpful to Lisa.

After reading Young's article, we engaged in the A/B Line activity. This activity further clarified the concept of oppression for the students. Trisha, a Japanese American student, wrote:

> This activity made oppression very clear to me. I know that if I walked into any store or place of business looking for employment, there is little chance that I wouldn't be hired. I never realized that for some people, not being able to find a job is an issue. [JN 11/12/02]

Courtney, an African American woman, pushed the discussion even further.

> During the discussion we discussed the United States as a "well-intentioned" society. I could not DISAGREE more! I see the

United States as a very DELIBERATELY OPPRESSIVE society where those in power are anything but "well intentioned" in terms of societal development. [JN 11/12/02]

In reflecting on students' writings and class discussions, I realized that students had difficulty understanding contemporary oppression. These difficulties arose because often they had a view of the concept that differed from the way it was being put forth in the class. At times, as in the case of Trisha, students believed that their life experiences were "just like everyone else's," and since they had not experienced oppression, maybe it wasn't an issue. On the other hand, those students who experienced contemporary oppression almost daily were often frustrated by other students' lack of understanding about what they deemed as "obvious."

It was important for me to effectively manage these opposing views and various stages of awareness. Neither Lisa, Trisha, nor Courtney needed to feel uncomfortable voicing her understanding of oppression in American society. All of these perspectives were the intellectual balls we juggled in class. This juggling did not necessitate reaching a common understanding. I did not think that was necessary at this stage of the students' development. What was important was a recognition that those perspectives co-existed in society. Students' knowledge of them could begin their process of learning how to respectfully address perspectives that differed from the ones they subscribed to, when they arose either in their classrooms or with members of the school community. Discussions of White privilege would prove an even more difficult concept for students to grasp.

***White Privilege.*** Peggy McIntosh (1988) describes White privilege as "an invisible package of unearned assets which I can count on cashing in each day, but about which I was 'meant' to remain oblivious" (p. 120). Discussions of concepts of White privilege also resulted in powerful classroom interactions. Texts such as "Confronting White Privilege" (Weiss, 2002), "Membership Has Its Privileges" (Wise, 2002), and "White Privilege, Color and Crime" (McIntosh, 1998), coupled with the activities such as Power Scatter, again took students through processes of resistance and realization. Lisa, who is White but grew up poor and stringently believed in meritocracy, strongly resented any notion of White privilege. First, in one activity, she had to acknowledge her socioeconomic status: "It was definitely more comforting to stand on the A line [advantage]. I couldn't help but notice almost every time I was on the B line [disadvantage] I was the only White person." After dealing with these differences, she was asked to consider herself as "privileged" in society. In week 5 of the course she wrote, "All my life I have not felt privileged" [JN 10/28/02]. However, in the following comments, she reflected on her new understanding of being privileged in a race-biased society:

> What I see now is that the privilege was imbedded in facets of my life that were invisible, like maybe the fact that I got a job when I was 15 over a person of color. Or maybe my family was able to rent the house we lived in because we were White. I had never thought of these things before. I don't want those advantages, but that would be impossible. An equal society along all lines seems like a joke! Its hard to admit these things. I'm privileged. There I said it! [JN 10/28/02]

After this realization came feelings of guilt for Lisa and other students with similar reflections.

At these times I could not answer the question of what to do with this guilt, in part because as an African American woman, I was very aware of the advantages of White privilege, and it was important for me that students who were advantaged by this bias in American society became consciously aware of such advantage. But how to get these students past feelings of guilt and helplessness is a challenge that still needs to be addressed by teacher educators, since merely acknowledging these feelings is not enough. Thankfully, other students in the room can become assets in these moments.

Shauna was extremely helpful to both me and other students, since her writing gave us a glimpse into what others might be feeling but were unable at the time to articulate. She wrote:

> I realize, however, that this helplessness comes from a desire to "fix it," to stabilize what has become unstable, so that I can return to my comfort zone. I'm in a constant struggle with the idea that dealing with these issues will *always* take me out of my "comfort zone." [JN 11/5/02]

Knowing more about the processes that students go through on the way to gaining and incorporating new and difficult meanings into their worldview is necessary if teacher educators are to become more competent themselves in facilitating students' journeys through such processes. Becoming a skilled facilitator in such classes is especially tantamount when the issue of racism is discussed in teacher education classes.

*Racism.* Tatum (1992) defines racism as "a system of advantage based on race" (p. 3). While students were able to grasp the injustice of overt racist acts, the systemic elements of racism were much harder to grasp. Similar to the notions of oppression, garnered from Young's discussion of contemporary oppression, and the subtleties of White privilege as discussed by McIntosh, students' realizations about White privilege as a corollary to racism was a difficult process. In this way, racism is highlighted as a system of *advantage* for some while also being a system of disadvantage for others.

When racism is seen as something that "bad/other" people do to minorities, students are willing and eager to take up the fight against racism. In this light, the fight against racism fits into their ethos of being American: fighting against injustice, fighting for those who can't fight for themselves. Every good American believes in these ideals and heartily can endorse such a cause.

However, realizing that the legacy of racism in America is a structure of inherited advantage for these same young White adults, the fight against racism is that much harder. This fight becomes one with the self when these young people realize that they may be on the wrong side of the argument, in that they are the perpetrators, not the defenders. They feel like hypocrites. With these realizations come guilt and a loss of the innocence of being solidly on the side of right. As Sarah, a White student, wrote:

> One thing that has been really hard for me is coming to grips with the fact that America is not this perfectly just and democratic society. I have always been someone who can be moved to tears by hearing a beautiful rendition of the national anthem because I have always felt such a love for America and have always felt so blessed to live here. I see now that there is still much improvement to be desired of America. I have been noticing things a lot more ever since this class began; things that offend me now that I think previously would have gone unnoticed. [JN 11/02/02]

All of a sudden, the subtle jokes, snide comments, exchanged looks—all based on a racist or discriminatory ideology to which these young people, and perhaps their friends and families, subscribed (and what they initially perceived only as a superficial, "We didn't mean anything by it; it was just a joke")—take on a deeper meaning as fleeting lenses to a worldview that informs their day-to-day interactions with people of different racial and cultural backgrounds from themselves. These young people began to re-examine their world: who their friends are, who's at the places where they hang out; which racial/ethnic groups are represented and in what capacity; and what their parents really think about minorities. This path of questioning leads to the greatest loss of all: the loss of a "safe" social network, a network of unconditional love.

This network is threatened because students, in an effort to start practicing these new competencies, start to challenge the worldview they hear around them to which they no longer want to subscribe. In most situations they are challenging the ones they love and who love them: their safety net against the world. And suddenly those who represent that safety net may begin to resent these new perspectives. Conflicts arise where before none existed. Values clash and ideological contradictions are exposed. Shauna's anguish was evident in her journal entry.

> My parents don't make racist remarks but my grandparents certainly do. They do not seem to recognize their racist implications, so how do I make them see it? How can I change a way of thinking that has been 80 years in the making? What questions do I ask? What comments do I make? How do you discuss those things without alienating them or causing irreparable rifts among loved ones? [JN 11/02/02]

My students started to experience a keen sense of isolation in the company of people with whom they used to feel the most comfortable. They really want to begin to live the new ideals they have embraced in class, but the price may be too high; while they are alienating all who currently love them, those whose cause they think they are fighting won't necessarily embrace them right away. They will be held in question in communities of color also, and when these moments occur, the isolation becomes even more intense.

What we have to teach our students is that the cause does not have to be an all-out fight in the beginning. In other words, students can tackle their use of these new competencies little by little. They can start in their classrooms and branch out to the school community, the community served by the school, and eventually their personal support community. Students should be encouraged to see that they are really fighting for the kind of world promised by society but that has not been delivered. Their cause is for their humanity and the humanity of their future biological children. The cause is to make sure that their children, when they first learn about the advantages of racism and privilege in their lives, don't experience the same sense of disillusionment about their parents and their country that they themselves feel. That's the cause. The cause is first for them and second for the children they will teach. But they will need help.

## HOW TO SEEK SUPPORT

I realized that although I encouraged my students to seek support in order to be successful in their classrooms, I had never taught them how to do so. Additionally, I never taught those students, who could be allies, the importance of being such a presence for their future colleagues. So I present these lessons here.

In Chapter 7 of this volume, Sleeter writes that, as a novice teacher, her overriding concern could have been, "How can I learn to assist my students to use academics as a tool for personal and collective advancement?" However, she noted that this was not her main concern. Instead, her overriding concern was about her "own comfort level in a multicultural or biracial context." This overriding concern was also evident in Shauna's and other students' writings, even though, at first glance, their concerns appeared to be about the students.

Thus, before seeking support, new teachers must be very honest with themselves. Ask yourself for whom you are seeking support—for yourself, to make you feel good about being in that particular school teaching those particular students? Or are you seeking support to better prepare yourself for the job of teaching? After all, this is a job that you chose, and therefore a choice for which you should need no affirmation. Teachers have to be honest because their tenacity, particularly in the face of adversity, depends on it. If teachers are looking for "feel good" moments to affirm their choice of school at which to teach, and these moments are not forthcoming as they would hope, they may, eventually, leave the profession. If, on the other hand, new teachers are looking for support to learn the best and most effective practices for a job to which they already are committed, they will find the support they need.

Once teachers have distinguished which type of support they are seeking, their job will become easier. To offer advice on seeking the latter type of support, I suggest starting with a teacher whose practices and pedagogy mirror his or her teaching aspirations. This person is already doing what the new teacher would like to do, and certainly will be able to guide the new teacher toward other sources of support, as this teacher's practices demonstrate that she seeks and gets support in her own process of development. In every urban school there is one or more of these mentor teachers, but to find/see them, new teachers, especially those from different racial and cultural backgrounds from their students, cannot hold on to preconceived notions about how mentor teachers should look or act. To find a racially and culturally competent mentor, a new teacher should observe colleagues through the eyes of their students and the interactions they have with students.

**Note:** Photo of Carl Grant © Michael John Streibel

## REFERENCES

McIntosh, P. (1989, July/August). White privilege: Unpacking the invisible knapsack. *Peace and Freedom*, 10–12

McIntosh, P. (1998). White privilege, color and crime: A personal account. In C. R. Mann & M. S. Zatz (Eds.), *Images of color, images of crime* (pp. 207–216). Los Angeles: Roxbury.

Obidah, J. E., & Teel, K. M. (2001). *Because of the kids: Facing racial and cultural differences in schools*. New York: Teachers College Press.

Tatum, B. D. (1992). Talking about race, learning about racism: The application of racial identity development theory in the classroom. *Harvard Educational Review, 62*(1), 1–24.

Weiss, D. (2002). Confronting white privilege. *Rethinking Schools, 14*(4). Retrieved July 29, 2002, from http://www.rethinkingschools.org/archives/16_04/conf164.htm

Wise, T. (2002). Membership has its privileges. *Rethinking Schools, 14*(4). Retrieved July 29, 2002, from http://www.rethinkingschools.org/archives/16_04/conf164.htm

Young, I. M. (2000). Five faces of oppression. In M. Adams, W. J. Blumenfeld, R. Castaneda, H. W. Hackman, M. Peters, & X. Zuniga (Eds.), *Readings for diversity and social justice: An anthology on racism, antisemitism, sexism, heterosexism, ableism and classism* (pp. 35–49). New York: Routledge.

# CHAPTER SIX

# Standing on the Rock: An African American Educator's Professional Development

*Kimberly Mayfield*

## THE FOUNDATION

### Before I Was Born

My parents, Aubrey Mayfield and Margie Gary Mayfield, were born in the segregated South in the 1930s. They grew up under Jim Crow, which sought to maintain the power structure of slavery (Takaki, 1993). After the Emancipation Proclamation of 1863, the Freedman's Bureau created schools to educate formerly enslaved Africans. By 1896, "separate but equal" facilities were sanctioned by federal law with the *Plessy v. Ferguson* ruling. Fifty-eight years later, the *Brown v. Board of Education* Topeka, Kansas, case would overturn *Plessy* and end legal segregation in schools (Watkins, 2001). However, before schools were desegregated, thousands of African Americans were educated in segregated schools. My parents are two examples of African Americans whose entire precollege education was spent in segregated schools.

My parents met at Monroe Colored High School in Monroe, Louisiana, in 1948. Their principal, Henry Carroll, always demanded the best from his students. The teachers at the school followed his lead and expected students to perform at their highest potential. Their goal was to provide students with a well-rounded high school experience. At Monroe Colored High School, students were reminded constantly of the value of education and encouraged to be the best at their chosen professions.

After my parents graduated from high school in 1952, they went to college. My mother attended the historically Black Grambling State College, while my father attended racially, culturally, and linguistically diverse colleges in San Francisco. After attending City College of San Francisco, my father earned a bachelor of science degree in biology from San Francisco State College in 1958. While my dad was in college, his father, R.P., became deathly ill. My father went to visit R.P. and was told explicitly not to let anything stand in the way of completing his education. R.P. also told my father that if he died, which he did, not to come home for the funeral, but to stay in school.

While at Grambling, my mother majored in elementary education. Her father, William, supported her financially. During the summer of her junior year, she learned that William did not have the money for her to return to school. She decided to stay home and work. Her mother, Louvella, had other plans. She had been saving money in a can under the house for new furniture. She gave the money to my mother to pay for her last year of college. My grandmother felt that if my mother stopped school to work, she would never find her way back. My mother graduated from Grambling State College in 1956 with a bachelor of science degree in elementary education. By this time, my grandfather was battling tuberculosis and was unable to attend my mother's graduation, but my grandmother was there.

## An Oakland State of Mind

I was born on November 28, 1966, in San Francisco, California, 7 years after my parents were married, and approximately 6 weeks after the Black Panther Party for Self Defense was founded in Oakland, California. When my parents bought a house in Oakland in 1967, members of the African American community were victimized by police brutality, denied membership in trade unions, and faced housing discrimination (Major, 2006). Huey P. Newton and Bobby Seal crafted the Ten-Point Program for the Black Panther Party for Self Defense on October 17, 1966 to address these issues.

My father was employed as an entomologist with the U.S Department of Agriculture in Albany, California, and my mother was hired as teacher in the Oakland Unified School District. I grew up experiencing many facets of middle-class life. My parents had jobs that gave them sick leave, annuities, steady paychecks, and health benefits. We vacationed in Michigan and Louisiana. I got braces, went to the dentist regularly, and went to the dermatologist and podiatrist as needed. I had my own telephone and got new clothes regularly. I had most of what I wanted and everything I needed.

I attended a small, private, racially and ethnically diverse school on the Oakland/Berkeley border named Twin Pines Day School from kindergarten through 6th grade. I went to school with extremely wealthy children and those who shopped at "Value Village," a second-hand clothing store. My classmates' parents held middle-class to upper-class jobs. Together we learned from a racially and culturally diverse curriculum. For example, we learned about Hanukkah, St. Patrick's Day, and Jackie Robinson breaking the race barrier in baseball. We studied Persia, Colonial America, and Africa. We sang Beatles songs and learned to play the ukulele and recorder. We also had lessons in Spanish, French, and ballet.

I was never taunted or teased because of my race or ethnic heritage at Twin Pines Day School. I was, however, teased significantly because of my weight, by the only other African American girl in my class. Although this chapter is about racial and cultural competence, I mention this experience because my White girlfriends always came to my defense. As an adult I learned that the teaser did so because she thought I wanted to be White.

I did not witness students being treated differently because of race or culture until I started public junior high and high school. I attended Bret Harte Junior High School in the Oakland Unified School District and Berkeley High School in the Berkeley Unified School District. Each school population was racially balanced with no clear racial or ethnic majority. However, tracking, as defined by Jeannie Oakes (1985), was blatantly apparent at both schools. The academically rigorous classes were populated with few African American and Latino students and mostly European American and Asian American students. The vocational classes were comprised of mostly African American and Latino students and few European American and Asian American students. I graduated from Berkeley High School fully prepared for college because my parents and I clearly communicated to my counselors that I was college bound and needed to be eligible to attend the University of California and California State University systems.

I began my freshman year at the University of California at Santa Barbara (UCSB) in 1984. All of my education to this point expertly prepared me for the racist, classist environment that I was entering.

My preparation came from a firm grounding in my identity as a self-assured African American woman with skills in racial and cultural competence. I knew how to get along with people from diverse racial, ethnic, socioeconomic, and linguistic backgrounds. UCSB's rich history of student protest and struggle was tempered with a profound aura of wealth and privilege. While I was a student at UCSB, the families of the students had the highest median income of all nine UC campuses. When I arrived at UCSB, the African American students were outraged at the university's handling of White fraternity members who had performed on stage in Black face. When confronted by several angry members of the African American student community, the performers replied that they did not know that what they did would offend anyone (Roberta Newton, personal communication, 2007). The university was slow to respond, but reprimanded the students in the summer when everyone was at home.

I earned a bachelor of arts degree in Black studies and political science in 1988 from the UCSB. After graduation, I traveled in Europe for 4 months. When I returned home, I was encouraged by one of my mother's friends to take the California Basic Educational Skills Test (CBEST) to become a teacher. My intention was to take a year off from school to work and apply to graduate school in American studies or political science. I did not have a clear professional goal when I completed my college degree. I thought I would become a psychologist or an attorney, but I did have fleeting thoughts of becoming a teacher.

### On the Faultline: The African American Educational Experience

When my parents were in school (elementary through high school), all of their teachers were African American. When my mother attended Grambling State College, all of her professors were African American. However, during the 1960s and 1970s, as schools were becoming desegregated, thousands of African American teachers were displaced (Walker, 1996). Black segregated schools were closed as students were sent to previously all-White schools. Presently, African American teachers represent 6% of the total teaching population (Nieto & Bode, 2007). However, African American students represent 17% of the national school-aged population (U.S. Department of Education, 2003a). Not only is the underrepresentation of African Americans noticeable in the teaching force; it is also acutely evident in the teacher education professorate.

European American professors represent the largest racial group in the field of education (U.S. Department of Education, 2004). Of the total education professorate, 83.1% is European American, while the remaining 16.9% comprises the following ethnic groups: 6.6% African American; 4.1% Asian or Pacific Islander; 3.3% Latino; and 2.9% American Indian or Alaskan Native or no race indicated (U.S. Department of Education, 2004). The shortage of faculty of color in the field of teacher education is significant because the professorate is not representative of national demographics or the demographics of the school-aged population. Currently 42% of school-aged children are from culturally and linguistically diverse backgrounds, while the majority of the education professorate is European American (U.S. Department of Education, 2003b, 2004). European Americans make up 80.3% of the total professorate, and people of African descent constitute 5.5% of the total professorate (U.S. Department of Education, 2004).

Scholars of African descent encounter many barriers when seeking employment, promotion, and tenure in institutions of higher education (Hendricks & Caplow, 1998; Turner & Myers, 2000). Research indicates that this may be due to the unwelcoming culture and climate of institutions of higher education for professors of diverse ethnic backgrounds (Solórzano, 1998). The lack of professors of African descent has a profound impact on the education of African American students and may negatively affect achievement (Irvine, 1989).

Teacher education and special education teacher training programs tend to be based on European American worldviews, beliefs, and values (Voltz, 1998). These perspectives may not create effective practices for teaching an increasingly culturally and linguistically diverse student population or lead teachers toward racial and cultural competence (Gollnick & Chinn, 1998). Teacher education and special education professors of African descent may positively impact the education of general education and special education credential candidates, by teaching through their cultural backgrounds and conducting research to improve educational equity and achievement for African American students throughout the educational continuum. Merryfield (2000) asserts that through their lived experiences, professors of color are positioned to move institutions of higher education beyond traditional paradigms to create an environment that will ensure educational equity for all students through social justice and antiracist, multicultural teacher education. A shortage of professors of African descent reduces the presence of ethnically diverse perspectives among teacher education professors. If professors of African descent remain untenured and feel unwelcome in institutions of higher education, their shortage in higher education may persist.

## MY RESEARCH

In two areas of my research (Mayfield, 2001), I investigated the employment experiences and perceptions of promotion and tenure among teacher education and special education professors of African descent at historically Black and traditionally White institutions of higher education ($n$ = 31). Data from a questionnaire with 20 Likert-type items, one open-ended question, and interviews ($n$ = 4) were analyzed. These sources of data addressed institutional racism, tenure and promotion expectations, feelings of tokenism, and teaching loads. Specifically, participants at traditionally White institutions said that they experienced institutional racism and felt that they had to work harder than their White colleagues during the rank and tenure process. These participants also indicated that they felt like they were selected to participate in various campus activities because of their racial identity. Participants at historically Black institutions reported having larger teaching loads more often than participants at traditionally White institutions. Overall, study participants reported that they were not recruited for positions in higher education while they were doctoral students, nor were they given mentors when they entered the education professorate.

## THE WILL TO SUCCEED: RACIAL AND
## CULTURAL COMPETENCE IN URBAN CLASSROOMS

My thoughts on racial and cultural competence in education come from watching my parents negotiate societal diversity after growing up in the segregated South, and my personal and professional educational experiences. I attended private and public schools from kindergarten through 12th grade in Oakland and Berkeley, California, with students who represented all areas of diversity. My college classmates were mostly European American and considerably wealthier than my junior high school and high school classmates. I have taught diverse students at the K–12 level, at the college level, and in teacher education programs. In my opinion, there are five characteristics, discussed below, that educators must aspire to as they journey towards racial and cultural competence.

### Critical Personal Reflection

Teachers bring their lived experiences into the classroom (hooks, 1994). They must recognize their personal biases and confront assumptions that may compromise their interactions with students from diverse backgrounds. European American teachers, specifically, must acknowledge and come to terms with their White skin privilege and understand the position it gives them in education and society.

### Willingness to Change

Teachers must be willing to change their perspectives on teaching and educational practice to meet the needs of their students. Currently, as stated earlier, 42% of school-aged children in America come from culturally and linguistically diverse backgrounds (U.S. Department of Education, 2003a). Conversely, 90% of the teachers are from European American backgrounds (Nieto & Bode, 2007). This discrepancy in backgrounds leads to a cultural mismatch between teachers and their students. Cultural mismatch is the misunderstanding or lack of understanding of different cultures (Hollins, 1996). Specifically, teachers with racial and cultural competence will employ culturally relevant strategies to teach and discipline students (Ladson-Billings, 1995) instead of using purely teacher-directed lessons and suspending misbehaving students.

### Promoting Student Success

Teachers must recognize that all parents want their children to be successful in school and in life, and all students want to be successful in school and in life. This reflects the basic human desire parents have for their children and students have for themselves. Teachers also should have this desire for their students. Sometimes teachers focus too much on their students' possible struggles (poverty, underperformance, giftedness, being an English language learner, etc.) and forget to look for their students' strengths (brilliance, enthusiasm, creativity, being questioning knowledge seekers).

## High Student Expectations

Teachers should expect all students to perform at their highest potential and be able to use culturally relevant strategies (Ladson-Billings, 1995) to get them there. Racially and culturally competent teachers successfully negotiate the line between honoring student backgrounds and getting them to perform at proficient academic levels. For example, a teacher may honor students' use of their home language and still require them to use standard English conventions in writing.

## Educational Activism

Teachers on the journey to racial and cultural competence must act when confronted with racism, prejudice, and discrimination in schools. These teachers must be willing to name what they see, critically reflect on incidents and act in ways to promote social justice (Freire, 1970). Explicitly, this means that teachers must recognize the injustice they witness, think of a strategy to combat the injustice, and use the strategy to change the outcome.

I offer the following example: When I was teaching at the K–12 level, I noticed that African American students were referred for special education services at a higher rate than students from other racial groups at my school. The resource specialist and I decided to develop an intervention program for students who were near the 50th percentile in reading and language arts on their standardized tests. We worked with the students in 6-week intervals. Pre- and posttesting measured student progress. At the end of the 6 weeks, we gave the students' teachers a profile of the reading and language arts strategies that we had used with the students. Over time, we were able to reduce the number of African American students who were assessed for special education services at our school.

## Personal Examples

In my mother's 37-year teaching career, she taught at one segregated school in Monroe, Louisiana, and at one desegregated school in Oakland, California. In both environments she approached teaching in the same way. She was completely committed to her students' academic success. She did not send students to the principal's office nor did she repeatedly call parents about misbehavior. She did not complain about what students did not have or did not know. She never felt that she had a student she could not teach. My mother developed racial and cultural competence skills during her teaching career through sheer determination. She was determined to ensure that all of her students experienced academic success.

I substitute taught in four Bay Area school districts before securing full-time employment. I worked as a self-contained special education teacher at a K–8 school in the Oakland Unified School District for 7 years. Because I was new to the teaching profession, I consulted my mother regularly. She supported me by sharing her lesson plans, classroom rituals, and activities. She even helped me cover my bulletin boards.

## MINING THE GOLD

Every day that I entered the classroom, I took the wisdom of my mother with me. I offer the following strategies for new and veteran teachers who teach diverse student populations that are largely African American and who are on the journey toward racial and cultural competence.

### Dress Professionally

My mother wore a dress or skirt, a girdle, stockings, and pumps every day of her teaching career in Monroe, Louisiana. She did not start to wear pants until the mid-1970s. In her 37-year teaching career, she never wore blue jeans to school. She always dressed the part of a professional. In doing so, she commanded respect from her students, parents, and administrators. Although I never really wore a girdle to school, I did always wear stockings and never wore blue jeans. Clothing may seem like a small thing, but it goes a long way in educational settings. Education is serious business for African Americans, and one way for teachers to convey understanding of this is to dress the part.

### Professional Preparation

My mother walked into the classroom prepared to teach every day. She was confident and organized. I learned to teach by trial and error, but my commitment to student learning was apparent. I prepared nightly, sometimes writing scripted lesson plans as a safety net for myself. African American students want to know that someone is in charge and knows what she is doing. Being prepared is the best way to illustrate this.

## Clear Parent Communication

My mother was always direct with parents about their children's academic performance. She let them know their children's strengths and weaknesses and always told them how to help their children at home. I mirrored this behavior in my teaching practice as well. I found that parents just wanted an unbiased assessment of how their children were doing in school. They also wanted to be sure that their children were being treated fairly in school. One way to communicate fairness is to regularly communicate accomplishments as well as challenges to parents.

## No Complaining

At Grambling State College, my mother was taught to take students where they were (e.g., do not lament about the information and skills that students do not have; rather, start at the students' skill levels and knowledge base and build from there) and teach them what they needed to know. This mind-set allows teachers to be effective with any student they encounter because they have a clear understanding of their professional responsibility. I chose to become a special education teacher because I wanted to prove that students who learn differently can, in fact, learn. Because of the learning profile of the students I had, there was no room for complaining, just action, just teaching.

## Pluralistic View of Culture

My mother did not teach students from diverse racial and cultural backgrounds until she started teaching in Oakland. However, because of her experiences with segregation, she knew firsthand what it meant to be excluded, devalued, and misjudged. I believe she was as effective with students from Latino, Asian, and European backgrounds as she was with African American students because of these experiences. My success with students from racially diverse backgrounds comes from my lived experiences. I was educated with students from diverse racial and cultural backgrounds and understood the value in difference. It is important to recognize that students are different without seeking to homogenize them.

### Effective Classroom Environment for Learning

My mother and I both had high academic expectations for all of our students. We felt that if they came to class, we could teach them what they needed to know. We held our students accountable for their learning and set high expectations for them. We told them they could learn; we taught and retaught concepts to them until they learned them. We also set clear behavioral goals for our students. We expected them to act like learners. We followed through on consequences. Neither of us regularly sent children to the office. We kept the locus of control in our classrooms. We knew that our parents were sending us the best children they had every morning. African American students and parents want to know that the teacher is in control of the classroom.

### Enjoy the Profession

My mother and I feel that teaching is a liberatory action. We believe that there is nothing more powerful than teaching someone to read or to excel in math. We loved our profession and it was evident in how we taught. Our students knew that we were passionate about our teaching and wanted to be in the classroom with them. Historically, in the African American community, teachers were highly respected because of the values they represented and the knowledge they acquired. I still believe this is true. Even though my mother retired in 1993, whenever she sees her former students, they proudly tell whomever they are with, "This is Mrs. Mayfield; she was my 1st-grade teacher."

## CONCLUDING STORY

In 2007, I reached a milestone in my teaching career. I attended the college graduation of one of the students in my first special education class. When we met in 1993, she was 9 years old and I was 27 years old. As we chatted after she received her diploma, through my tears of joy and pride, I congratulated her, and she thanked me for being a role model for her. I asked her if she remembered me telling her when she was younger that she could achieve any goal she set for herself. She smiled and said yes.

**Note:** Photo of Kimberly Mayfield by Karen Manheim Teel.

## REFERENCES

Freire, P. (1970). *Pedagogy of the oppressed.* New York: Continuum.

Gollnick, D. M., & Chinn, P. C. (1998). *Multicultural education in a pluralistic society.* Upper Saddle River, NJ: Merrill.

Hendricks, A. D., & Caplow, J. A. (1998, November). *African American faculty perceptions of the academic culture and their professional socialization.* Paper presented at the annual meeting of the Association for the Study of Higher Education, Miami, FL.

Hollins, E. R. (1996). *Culture in school learning: Revealing the deep meaning.* Mahwah, NJ: Erlbaum.

hooks, b. (1994). *Teaching to transgress: Education as the practice of freedom.* New York: Routledge.

Irvine, J. J. (1989). Beyond role models: An examination of cultural influences on the pedagogical perspectives of black teachers. *Peabody Journal of Education, 66*(4), 51–63.

Ladson-Billings, G. (1995). But that's just good teaching! The case for culturally relevant pedagogy. *Theory Into Practice, 34,* 159–165.

Major, R. (2006). *A panther is a black cat: An account of the early years of the Black panther party—its origins, its goals and its struggle for survival.* Baltimore: Black Classics Press

Mayfield, K. (2001). *Coming to voice: The experiences of professors of African descent in historically Black and traditionally White institutions of higher education.* Unpublished doctoral dissertation, University of San Francisco.

Merryfield, M. M. (2000). Why aren't teachers being prepared to teach for diversity, equity, and global interconnectedness? A study of lived experiences in the making of multicultural and global educators. *Teaching and Teacher Education, 16,* 429–443.

Nieto, S., & Bode, P. (2007). *Affirming diversity: The social political context of multicultural education* (5th ed.). Boston: Pearson Education.

Oakes, J. (1985). *Keeping track: How schools structure inequality.* New Haven, CT: Yale University Press.

Solórzano, D. G. (1998). Critical race theory, race and gender micro-aggressions, and the experience of Chicana and Chicano scholars. *International Journal of Qualitative Studies in Education, 11*(1), 21–136.

Takaki, R. (1993). *A different mirror: A history of multicultural America.* New York: Little, Brown.

Turner, C.S.V., & Myers, S. L. (2000). *Faculty of color in academe.* Needham Heights, MA: Allyn & Bacon.

U.S. Department of Education. (2003a). National Education Statistics, Common Core Data, Public Elementary/Secondary School Universe Survey, 1998–2003. Washington, DC: Author.

U.S. Department of Education. (2003b). National Education Statistics, Integrated Post Secondary Data System (IPEDS), Winter 2003–04. Washington, DC: Author.

U.S. Department of Education. (2004). National Education Statistics, National Study of Post Secondary Faculty (NSOPF:04). Washington, DC: Author.

Voltz, D. L. (1998). Cultural diversity and special education teacher preparation: Critical issues confronting the field. *Teacher Education and Special Education*, 21(1), 63–70.

Walker, V. (1996). *Their highest potential: An African American school community in the segregated south.* Chapel Hill: University of North Carolina Press.

Watkins, W. H. (2001). *The white architects of black education: Ideology and power in America, 1865–1954.* New York: Teachers College Press.

# CHAPTER SEVEN

# Learning to Become a Racially and Culturally Competent Ally

*Christine Sleeter*

> My friends of color are skeptical of those of
> us who are white and who talk of change and
> diversity. We have made mistakes over these
> years; have promised action and stayed with
> discussion. . . . Yet despite all of this history,
> and despite my own daily mistakes, I still be-
> lieve in the power of white activism. . . . I can
> begin to form alliances.
> —Julie Landsman, 2001, pp. 153–154

## RACE RELATIONS FROM A WHITE PERSPECTIVE

White people have a long history of, at best, getting in the way of
the progress of people of color and, more generally, reinforcing and
benefiting from everyday racism. In education, for example, there is
ample evidence that White people enter the teaching profession bringing little or no understanding of race and racism, but well-armed with
misinformation and stereotypes learned over the years (Barry & Lechner, 1995; Marx, 2003; Richman et al., 1997; Schultz, Neyhart, & Reck,
1996; Smith, Mollem, & Sherrill, 1997; Terrill & Mark, 2000). After all,
Whites are the most segregated and isolated racial category in the
United States (Orfield & Lee, 2005). We assume we can teach anyone,
but at the same time routinely carry stereotypes into the classroom

that support deficit thinking and depressed expectations for academic learning of students of color, particularly African American students (Avery & Walker, 1993; Irvine & York, 1993; Pang & Sablan, 1998; Tettegah, 1996). What does it mean, then, to become a White racially and culturally competent teacher of African American students? Does one actually *become* a competent ally, or, as Landsman suggests above, is it more honest to say that one works at it, gradually becoming more dependable?

Growing up in an all-White town in southern Oregon, I began life unprepared to become racially and culturally competent. I have few memories in which, as a child, I noticed race because usually everyone around me was White. In one of those few memories in which race came to the forefront, my family was visiting relatives in the San Francisco area. As we drove along, an aunt gave a negative running commentary about African American people we passed. Uncomfortable with her words, I finally challenged how she could say such things about people she did not know personally. She reprimanded me, saying, "Christine, you didn't grow up with them, so you don't know. I *did* grow up with them." My mother had taught me not to make judgments about people without getting to know them first. Violating that teaching did not feel right to me, but at the time, I was not acquainted with anyone who was not White, so I remained silent.[1]

In this chapter, I use stories of my growth to illustrate learning processes that are common among White educators, situating these stories within racial identity development theory. According to Helms (1990), "The term 'racial identity' actually refers to a sense of group or collective identity based on one's perception that he or she shares a common racial heritage with a particular racial group" (p. 3). Thompson and Carter (1997) stress that "the experience of peeling away the layers of societal racism and the concomitant self-reflection entailed in understanding one's racial identity" is a very difficult and long-term project that challenges one's conception of self and the world (p. xv). Racial identity development theory posits stages marked by shifts in perspective and self-identity as people move from seeing unequal race relations as "normal," to working actively for racial justice and equity.

Whites and people of color experience racial identity development differently due to occupying very different positions in the racial order and, consequently, having very different experiences with racism. I will be using racial identity development theory here as it relates to

Whites. As Frankenberg (1993) put it, seemingly idiosyncratic strategies through which White individuals interpret race are, in fact, "linked to a larger picture, whether consciously or not" (p. 144). This larger picture characterizes our view of the social world, the stratified nature of that world, and the way we make sense of the social location of people like ourselves. Although these stages often are discussed as linear, people do not automatically proceed through them, or necessarily follow a linear pattern. As one struggles with racism, one becomes better and better at recognizing and challenging it in a morally defensible and effective way, but one does not "arrive" at a point beyond which there is nothing left to learn or struggle with.

In what follows, I offer glimpses into viewpoints, struggles, and limitations I experienced that characterize my work with African American students. My hope is that, as White people see themselves in one another's stories, we will be able to move one another forward toward becoming increasingly reliable racially and culturally competent allies.

## WHAT DO "THEY" THINK ABOUT ME?

As I looked around at the faces in my student teaching classroom, I found myself wanting to be accepted. This was 10th-grade "world history" in an inner-city school. The students looking back at me represented a rainbow of diversity. Whites were definitely outnumbered; even my cooperating teacher, a middle-aged Asian American, wasn't White.

This was not my first experience being in the numerical minority. I had lived in Japan for a summer while in college, so I had experienced standing out, being stared at, not fitting in. But I was not used to being in the presence of a significant number of African Americans (who constituted about 30% of my student teaching class), nor did I even have terminology to describe the other non-White students. (Oriental was out, but what was acceptable? Spanish wasn't right, but what was correct? And what about students of mixed racial backgrounds?) The year was 1971. I was sufficiently aware of the Civil Rights Movement to know that racism characterized Black–White relationships, but I was terribly ignorant about the nature of racism or how White people were positioned within it, except as the "bad guys." I wanted to be a "good" White.

Helms (1990) points out that White people at the stage of *contact* see people of color, but assume the existing racial order to be normal. Having learned that racism is a taboo topic for discussion, as I had, Whites generally grow up terribly ignorant of it and see it as a thing of the past (Tatum, 1992). They believe and have internalized racial stereotypes that justify why Whites tend to be better off than people of color, usually using "color-evasive and power-evasive" thinking (Frankenberg, 1993, p. 14). At the *contact* stage, White people often maintain a sense of self-esteem and hold "positive feelings about the 'idea' of Blacks" (Helms, 1990, p. 57), not yet having learned how racism systemically privileges Whites and consequently defining racism as interpersonal prejudice only.

As a novice teacher, my overriding concern could have been: How can I learn to assist my students to use academics as a tool for personal and collective advancement? But it wasn't. Throughout my early teaching experience in the inner city, my overriding concern was: Do the students like me, and especially, do the students of color like me? At the earliest stages of racial identity development, this question focuses on oneself and one's own comfort level in a multiracial or biracial context. A White person who is unaccustomed to working with African American students (or other students of color) is often afraid of being perceived as racist and looks to the students for confirmation that he or she is one of the "good" White people.

This was true in my case. I talked with the students both inside and outside of class. Since I lived near the school and occasionally ran into some of them on the street, on occasion I invited them to my apartment to talk or just hang out. In the process of getting to know my students, I learned about one young man's mixed-race background, a couple of young men's interest in the National Basketball Association, young women's fashion preferences, and many of the students' music tastes. I also came to see the irrelevance of the world history textbook to their everyday lives. So, when it was my turn to teach, I co-planned with the students a student-centered cooperative learning unit about women's liberation (a topic the students chose). As I helped students dig into subtopics they chose for research, I learned that inner-city students need not necessarily find school boring—my students found the unit we co-designed to be quite engaging.

But never once during the months I spent in that school did I, or adults within earshot of me, consider what the students might do after graduation and what kind of academic preparation they might need, especially if they were to attend higher education. When I replaced study of the world history text with my student-centered unit, it did not occur to me to wonder whether I might be shortchanging students' preparation for college or how I might strengthen their preparation. When chatting with the students informally, I asked about their interest in sports, fashion, or music, but not about what they might do after high school graduation. Although I would continue to teach in urban secondary schools, it would be at least another 2 years before these questions emerged. The relationships I formed with the students of color were enjoyable and educative for me, but, in retrospect, served me more than them. The fact that the students warmed up to me helped reassure me that I must not be one of the racist White people. I suspect that occupying the role of teacher further hinders noticing systemic privilege, since teachers usually occupy a higher status than students. I could attribute my access to resources and privileges my students lacked to my status as a teacher rather than my race.

In my work with teachers over the years, I often have heard White teachers refer to their good personal relationships with students of color as evidence that they are not racist, and sometimes as evidence that I am exaggerating the significance of racism in schools today. When a White teacher develops personal relationships with African American students, it is possible that he or she will not be jolted out of the *contact* stage if those relationships appear to confirm that he or she isn't racist. Yet for the students, those relationships may well not lead anywhere. Stanton-Salazar (1997) points out that relationships with teachers potentially can serve students as a form of social capital to navigate up the social structure. But for "low-status children," such relationships usually do not serve that purpose because so often White teachers view students as lacking academic ability.

My relationships with the students led me to stay in the urban school district. Over the next years, interaction with African American adults I befriended gradually led to *disintegration* of many racist assumptions. *Disintegration* is Helms's (1990) term for White people's initial recognition of racism.

## WHAT DO I KNOW ABOUT THEM?

By the mid-1970s, I was a learning disabilities teacher in a desegregated high school north of the inner-city area. I was living in a mixed

Black–White neighborhood on the edge of the inner city, spending most of my free time with a mixed Black–White group of friends. My boyfriend, an African American who worked with the city's desegregation program, played on a racially mixed, African American-sponsored softball team. Since the other teams they played were White, his was viewed as the Black team. For about 3 years I rarely missed a game. In the context of softball tournaments, barbecues, parties, and everyday life events, I found my identity and view of the world undergoing a profound shift.

I learned that the Civil Rights Movement had not ended racial discrimination. As I watched African American friends struggle to locate decent housing, avoid dangerous White communities outside the city, drive further to buy groceries than I was used to driving, and deal with police surveillance on a daily basis, I gradually learned what institutional racism is. As I listened to African American friends debrief at the end of the day, I learned that racism was a common topic of conversation in which people shared experiences and strategies for coping. (In my experience growing up, racism had never been a topic of conversation among White people.) Through listening, I also learned a good deal about the everyday workings of racism, as well as cultural nuances. By asking questions, I learned things such as how to interpret Black students' nonverbal behavior in the classroom or how to interpret various family structures.

Becoming aware of racism, especially as one becomes older, can be immensely painful, prompting feelings of anger and guilt, which trigger reactions that range from anger, to withdrawal from the situation, to searching for an immediate solution to "fix" racism. For me, *disintegration* was less traumatic than it is for many Whites, probably because, rather than dismissing my naive questions, African American friends patiently answered them.

At the same time, I immersed myself in bits of Black urban culture—music (Marvin Gaye, Stevie Wonder, the Isley Brothers), movies (*Shaft* and *Superfly*), food (barbecue, ham hocks, cornbread, greens), and dance forms. I was oil painting at the time; Black people graced my canvasses, and African American friends became recipients of completed projects. According to Helms (1990), Whites generally cope with the discomfort of *disintegration* either by continuing to learn or by reverting to earlier perspectives, which she termed *reintegration*. Tatum (1992) argues that continued support can help a White person avoid regressing and instead move toward *pseudo-independence,* a stage of continued learning about racism and acceptance of responsibility for maintaining or disrupting it. However, at that stage, learning is mainly at an intellectual level. The White person has rejected an earlier racist identity, but has not yet constructed an alternative, so instead may try on a "colorized" identity, such as using Black English or wearing non-White ethnic identity symbols.

As I learned to see the society I had grown up in from the other side of the color line, my identity shifted. No longer did I identify with the White town I had grown up in, since for my African American friends, White spaces were often dangerous and the White people there were ignorant. Unclear how to identify as White, but clearly not Black, I briefly adopted elements of a Black identity, such as carrying a hair pick and trying out a bit of African American language. Such *pseudo-independent* expressions of identity can be ridiculous, however; as Helms (1990) points out, other White people reject them and Black people are suspicious of them. One of my mother's best friends dismissed me as trying to be Black. Several Black women I encountered regarded me as a White threat who was out to steal Black men. For a time, I struggled with the dilemma of not being able to return to my old White self, but not seeing an alternative White self to become.

A turning point occurred when I decided to form a "Rainbow" group of teachers in my high school. Modeled in part after a multiracial group of educators who were writing some of the first multicultural curriculum to help schools with desegregation, I envisioned my group as identifying aspects of racism in our high school that we could work to change. Until I left for doctoral study at the end of that academic year, about eight young teachers of diverse racial backgrounds met in my classroom periodically to generate an action agenda. We discussed problems such as the Whiteness of the curriculum, the marginalized position African American students occupied in the school, and perceptions that the desegregation plan had compromised the school's academic quality. To take action, we organized a workshop for our colleagues to introduce them to strategies for integrating the curriculum (these were simplistic strategies, having been borrowed from elementary school human relations activities).

This work was significant to my growth in two ways. First, through it I was able to see myself as a White educator working collaboratively with colleagues of color to address racism in my school. The multiracial group of educators I had modeled my teacher group after included

White people, giving me glimmerings of what an antiracist White identity might be. In creating a group in my school, I began to take up that identity. Second, I began to read more intentionally about race and ethnicity than I had earlier. Rather than relying primarily on people of color to teach me about themselves, I became a more self-directed reader. For example, after identifying Mexican Americans as a group I knew nothing about, I started reading some of the emergent Chicano studies books such as *Occupied America* (Acuña, 1972).

*Immersion* refers to the process of seeking out and learning about alternative antiracist White identities and forms of constructive action (Helms, 1990). Role models, autobiographies, or histories of moral ancestors—other White people who have learned to work for social justice and have constructed an alternative White identity—are particularly important resources for learning (Christensen, 2000; Tatum, 1994). A danger of the *immersion* stage, however, is that continued focus on one's own group can end up re-creating White dominance. White studies literature and courses, for example, can take a form through which Whites again take over the discourse on multiculturalism (Sheets, 2000).

Ultimately, to be useful in disrupting racism, White allies of people of color need to reach a stage of *autonomy*, which entails long-term commitment to take on the work of struggling for racial justice. People at the *autonomy* stage can collaborate productively with others of diverse racial backgrounds to reduce racism in systems around us. *Autonomy*, however, is not a finished end state, but rather an ongoing process of learning.

## BECOMING RACIALLY AND CULTURALLY COMPETENT

Fast-forward 2 decades, to when I am a faculty member in a very diverse university. A student paper I am reading is decent, but not great. I could give it a "B" grade and move on. Or I could help the student strengthen the paper, in the process assisting her in developing academic tools she might use in doctoral study. Although I am not certain she has considered doctoral study, I can tell from talking with her that she is very bright, has good ideas, and has motivation. So, I take the time to write detailed comments on her paper. I return it to her the next day with a note encouraging her to consider going on for a doctorate and an invitation to rewrite this paper in preparation.

Incidents like this happen all the time. An educator sees potential in a student and decides to spend extra time and effort mentoring her or him. But this is more likely to happen to White students than to students of color. For a variety of reasons, African American students in higher education (the level at which I now work), particularly women, are the most isolated group of students on predominantly White campuses, receiving less mentoring than other students (Ellis, 2000; Fleming, 1984). African American faculty are in short supply, and White faculty members often have lower expectations for African American than White students. Further, faculty members in general—without necessarily thinking about it—gravitate toward students they understand and feel most comfortable with, who are often similar to themselves (Stanley & Lincoln, 2005). As a result, White students tend to get more faculty mentoring than do students of color. Students of color often report more satisfaction with mentors of their own race (Ortiz-Walters & Gilson, 2005; Santos & Reigadas, 2002), but the quality of a supportive, trusting relationship matters more than race (Lee, 1999).

The student paper I mentioned above was written by an African American student.[2] As when I had student-taught, I continue to ground my work in personal relationships with students and to invite them to co-construct some of the curriculum with me. However, unlike earlier, I have learned to situate teaching within an analysis of culture and racism (as well as other forms of difference and oppression), particularly as manifest in education. Further, I have learned to take on constructive work addressing racism in education.

For example, I had become aware of racial and gender disparities in access to mentoring shortly after earning my doctorate. At conferences I often initiated conversations by asking people what they were working on. A pattern quickly emerged in the nature of responses I received. White men who recently had earned their doctorates usually described various research projects in which they were involved and mentioned established faculty members with whom they were working. Faculty members of color who recently had earned their doctorates, on the other hand—particularly women—rather quickly shifted the conversation from what they were working on to their frustrations with professional isolation. I heard story after story about good ideas for research and interesting dissertation work, coupled with invisibility within networks of mostly White colleagues. Such conversations suggest antiracist roles for White faculty.

One such role involves academic mentoring. Having been well mentored myself (by an African American faculty member), I learned to write successfully for publication and to navigate the academic publishing world. While editing my first book, I learned to coach other new scholars on their academic writing. When I was invited to edit a book series, I jumped at the chance. Having been offered a "gatekeeper" role, I reflected on who was most and least likely to be let in, based on not only an understanding of institutional racism but also my personal conversations with junior faculty members. I saw this as an opportunity to open doors that otherwise might not be opened to junior scholars, particularly those of color. While editing the series, my queries regarding what junior faculty members were working on often led to book contracts. Over a period of about 15 years, 30 books were published in the series. Sixteen are by authors of color who mainly needed someone with access to publishing to take their work seriously and give critical feedback on it along with encouragement and support.[3]

Another such role involves institutional transformation. I continued to learn to use an "equity lens" to work toward transforming education institutions so they support everyone. My ability to do this effectively improved gradually with practice and benefited over the years from student critiques. I recall having designed and taught a multicultural education course for several years in a preservice teacher education program in which the great majority of students were White. Near the end of one semester, the only African American student in the class commented that the course addressed appropriate issues for White students to deal with, but offered African American students too little they didn't already know. Her comment caused me to reflect on the fact that I was teaching as if all of the students were White. A subsequent experience teaching much the same course to a cohort of preservice students of color enabled me to see better how to intellectually stretch students of diverse racial and ethnic backgrounds. Based on ongoing feedback from the students regarding what they already knew and what they wanted to study in more depth, I modified the course as we went along. For example, since they already knew a good deal about institutional racism, we skipped introductory analysis of it and moved to complex examinations of how institutional racism in schools can be challenged.

In 1997, after moving to California, I worked with faculty colleagues to initiate a master of arts in education program that had the explicit intent of offering an academically challenging curriculum that grounded diverse teacher-leaders in multicultural social justice education (see Sleeter et al., 2005).[4] Six years later, we successfully had attracted and graduated about four cohorts that mirrored the racial diversity of California. A racially diverse group of faculty ourselves, we created a program that featured a critical multicultural curriculum, oriented around action research for school transformation. Of the 49 students who had graduated by 2003, 49% were of color, 10% were international, and 41% were White American, a record that contrasts with California's average of 70% of its master's degrees going to Whites in a state in which 47% of the population is White. Although the institution in which we built this program was structured and funded largely as a teaching institution, we conceptualized the program as having a rigorous academic core so that its graduates would be able to use their degree for doctoral study if they so chose. At the time of this writing, about seven of the 49 who had graduated by 2003 (mostly people of color) are working toward doctorates and two have completed doctorates.

We also worked to transform various components of the program that often embodied, implicitly or explicitly, White privilege, as well as other forms of privilege (such as class, gender, and language). For example, we designed curriculum in which students of color found themselves well represented in readings. All courses (carrying titles such as Culture, Cognition, and Development; Technology as a Tool for Equity; Biliteracy; and Multicultural Curriculum Design) made explicit the importance of culture to teaching and learning. We went beyond making the readings multicultural, however, by basing main ideas in each course on our familiarity with research and perspectives from the margins, including African American perspectives on education. The program's introductory course, for instance, explored the sociopolitical context of schools, helping students to locate their work, interests, and goals in larger discourses about social justice, education, and research.

Yet another role for White allies is to support other White people who are learning to challenge racism. I don't consciously think of myself as a role model, but White students often remind me that I serve in that capacity. Several years ago, teachers from one of my classes decided to attempt to form a local activist organization. I encouraged a White teacher friend who had been one of my students to join. Although the group never quite jelled,[5] the time I spent with her helped her see how I deal with conflict over ideas in multiracial contexts in which I am not "the expert" just because of my status as professor.

During one meeting, the group engaged in a heated debate over models of school reform for low-income students of color. As we drove home, the White teacher commented that it must have been difficult for me to be attacked. I almost stopped the car, I was so surprised. What I had interpreted as a discussion in which people were able to disagree openly and passionately, she had interpreted as an attack. But I had not felt attacked. I told her that from my point of view, the fact that we could disagree and debate, then come to some agreement about what to do next, was constructive. My ideas had been listened to; some had been accepted and others had been questioned. That was part of the process. My teacher friend commented that her skin wasn't yet as thick as mine, and she wondered if she could engage in activist work. A year later, she turned up as one of the few White teachers in an activist group that initiated her district's first dual immersion bilingual school. I smiled to myself: She had learned that solidarity is built through passionate debates and disagreements in which White people can be a part, but are never exempt from critique and challenge.

## CONCLUSION

Racial and cultural competence is a relative state, not a final point of arrival. *Autonomy* for White people is an ongoing process of learning, and engaging in this process does not bring about perfection or completion (Helms, 1990). White people are always beneficiaries of racism. No matter how aware we are, we sometimes fail to notice privileges we receive; we sometimes miss opportunities to intervene or support. In class, for instance, occasionally I miss student comments I should have addressed. Do I miss them because of White insensitivity, or because my attention is focused on something else? When giving critical feedback to students, I sometimes forget their vulnerabilities and end up discouraging rather than encouraging. Do I forget because I'm actually trying to weed out the student, or because I assume trust when it hasn't yet been built?

Yet, for White people, the alternative is becoming bystanders who tacitly accept White supremacy as well as other forms of oppression. There is no comfortable way to grapple with race and racism. But the pleasure I have found in relationships with a wide diversity of people, including both students and colleagues of diverse backgrounds, has outweighed and continues to outweigh the ongoing pain and discomforts of acknowledging, continuing to learn about, and continuing to challenge racism.

## NOTES

1. Ironically, on the basis of DNA testing a year ago, I learned that I have about 6% African American ancestry. One of my grandmothers, the mother of this aunt, would have been about one-quarter Black. In the context of Jim Crow, the story of her dark complexion was altered somewhere along the line to claim that she was part Cherokee. I suspect that neither my mother nor my aunt ever knew the truth.

2. Although I was thinking about one of my African American students when describing the student paper, many of my White students, as well as my students from other backgrounds, will recognize themselves as recipients of the same treatment.

3. Twenty of the thirty books were authored by women. The series, Social Context of Education, published by SUNY Press, ended by mutual agreement when my immensely supportive editor and friend Priscilla Ross retired from SUNY Press.

4. Although at the time of this writing the program is still in existence, most of us who designed it are no longer at that institution, and the program has fallen into a state of disrepair.

5. After several meetings, the group fell apart because we were too scattered geographically. We tried to accommodate geographic dispersion by holding each meeting in a different community, with the unintended result that different people came to each meeting, so the group developed no continuity and cohesion.

## REFERENCES

Acuña, R. (1972). *Occupied America: The Chicano's struggle toward liberation.* San Francisco: Canfield Press.

Avery, P. G., & Walker, C. (1993). Prospective teachers' perceptions of ethnic and gender differences in academic achievement. *Journal of Teacher Education, 44*(1), 27–37.

Barry, N. H., & Lechner, J. V. (1995). Preservice teachers' attitudes about and awareness of multicultural teaching and learning. *Teaching and Teacher Education, 11*(2), 149–161.

Christensen, L. (2000). Creating a vision of possibility. *Rethinking Schools, 15*(1). Retrieved November 15, 2007, from http://www.rethinkingschools. org/archive/15_01/Rrr151.shtml

Ellis, E. M. (2000, Fall). Race, gender and the graduate student experience: Recent research. *Diversity Digest*. Retrieved July 25, 2006, from http://www.diversityweb.org/Digest/F00/contents.html

Fleming, J. (1984). *Blacks in college*. San Francisco: Jossey-Bass.

Frankenberg, R. (1993). *The social construction of whiteness: White women, race matters*. Minneapolis: University of Minnesota Press.

Helms, J. E. (1990). *Black and white racial identity*. Westport, CT: Greenwood Press.

Irvine, J. J., & York, D. E. (1993). Teacher perspectives: Why do African American, Hispanic, and Vietnamese students fail? In S. E. Rothstein (Ed.), *Handbook of schooling in urban America* (pp. 161–173). Westport, CT: Greenwood Press.

Landsman, J. (2001). *A white teacher talks about race*. Lanham, MD: Scarecrow Press.

Lee, W. Y. (1999). Striving toward effective retention: The effect of race on mentoring African American students. *Peabody Journal of Education, 74*(2), 27–43.

Marx, S. (2003). Entanglements of altruism, whiteness, and deficit thinking. *Education for Urban Minorities, 2*(2), 41–46.

Orfield, G., & Lee, C. (2005). *Why segregation matters*. Boston: Harvard University Civil Rights Project.

Ortiz-Walters, R., & Gilson, L. L. (2005). Mentoring in academia: An examination of the experiences of protégés of color. *Journal of Vocational Behavior, 67*(3), 459–475.

Pang, V. O., & Sablan, V. A. (1998). Teacher efficacy. In M. E. Dilworth (Ed.), *Being responsive to cultural differences* (pp. 39–58). Washington, DC: Corwin Press.

Richman, C. L., Bovelsky, S., Kroovand, N., Vacca, J., & West, T. (1997). Racism 102: The classroom. *Journal of Black Psychology, 23*(4), 378–387.

Santos, S., & Reigadas, E. T. (2002). Latinos in higher education: An evaluation of a university faculty mentoring program. *Journal of Hispanic Higher Education, 1*(1), 40–50.

Schultz, E. L., Neyhart, K., & Reck, U. M. (1996). Swimming against the tide: A study of prospective teachers' attitudes regarding cultural diversity and urban teaching. *Western Journal of Black Studies, 20*(1), 1–7

Sheets, R. H. (2000). Advancing the field or taking centre stage: The white movement in multicultural education. *Educational Researcher, 29*(9), 15–21.

Sleeter, C., Hughes, B., Meador, E., Whang, P., Rogers, L., Blackwell, K., Laughlin, P., & Peralta-Nash, C. (2005). Working an academically rigorous, multicultural program. *Equity & Excellence in Education, 38*(4), 290–299.

Smith, R., Mollem, M., & Sherrill, D. (1997). How preservice teachers think about cultural diversity. *Educational Foundations, 11*(2), 41–62.

Stanley, C. A., & Lincoln, Y. A. (2005). Cross-race faculty mentoring. *Change, 37*(2), 44.

Stanton-Salazar, R. D. (1997). A social capital framework for understanding the socialization of racial minority children and youths. *Harvard Educational Review, 67*(1), 1–40.

Tatum, B. D. (1992). Talking about race, learning about racism: An application of racial identity development theory in the classroom. *Harvard Educational Review, 52*(1), 1–24.

Tatum, B. D. (1994). Teaching White students about racism: The search for White allies and the restoration of hope. *Teachers College Record, 95*(4), 462–476.

Terrill, M., & Mark, D. L. H. (2000). Preservice teachers' expectations for schools with children of color and second-language learners. *Journal of Teacher Education, 51*(2), 149–155.

Tettegah, S. (1996). The racial consciousness attitudes of White prospective teachers and their perceptions of the teachability of students from different racial/ethnic backgrounds: Findings from a California study. *Journal of Negro Education, 65*(2), 151–163.

Thompson, C. E., & Carter, R. T. (Eds.). (1997). *Racial identity theory.* Mahwah, NJ: Erlbaum.

# CHAPTER EIGHT

# Makin' It Real: Rethinking Racial and Cultural Competence in Urban Classrooms

*Tarika Barrett*
*Pedro A. Noguera*

### ADOPTING A LENS

Much of the research related to issues of cultural competence has focused on the role that individual teachers can play in coming to know and value the cultural heritages and unique communities of their students (Gay, 2000; Irvine, 2003; Lipman, 1995; Sleeter, 2001). We agree that promoting racial and cultural competence among teachers is an important piece in the larger effort to address the many pressing issues related to the education of children who historically have been marginalized in American schools. However, it is our contention that much of the existing literature in multicultural education narrowly frames racial and cultural competence as a matter of understanding the culture of children in terms of racial identity, heritage, and family background. While such information may provide prospective teachers with important background information, it rarely provides the insights they will need to be successful in the classroom. This is because most approaches to multicultural education, and teacher education generally, ignore a more fundamental and existential question about the lives of students we teach: What knowledge and skill are required to successfully educate the children we serve? As simple as this question might seem, working with teachers to find answers to it compels those who educate teachers to engage them in new and different ways.

In this chapter we share insights about how our own experiences in the field of education have shaped how we understand what it means to develop "racial and cultural competence" as educators. We do not believe that the work of fostering a genuinely multicultural learning community, where an individual student's race, language, and culture are honored, should ever be couched in terms that allow educators to believe that they have "arrived" and successfully have created these ideal spaces for the students they teach. Like the constant flux in the communities and contexts in which students reside, our willingness to acknowledge our inability to ever completely "know" our students must drive us to come to see teaching as an ongoing process of learning.

We devote some of the chapter to a discussion of what it means to know and serve students of color. As we think about the relationships that teachers form with their students, we ask whether knowing the race and cultural backgrounds of our students is enough to lead to improved academic outcomes. Other questions we raise address how educators avoid the pitfalls of subscribing to racial or cultural stereotypes that guide how they interact with their students. How exactly can teachers engage in reflexivity around issues of race in a way that is edifying for them and their students? Finally, what can teachers do to understand the worldview and lived experience of students whose lives are so different from their own? These are just some of the questions we address.

Our goal is to provide teachers with a way of thinking about the concept of racial and cultural competence. We anticipate that the stories we share will resonate with educators who, despite years of experience, have encountered similar challenges in working successfully with marginalized students. We advocate that teachers adopt a stance of inquiry that will help them navigate these experiences.

## THE TEACHER AS ANTHROPOLOGIST: LEARNING ABOUT STUDENTS' CULTURES

### Tarika's Personal Entry Point

"Jamaica is the country that has given me all that I am." This was what my mother told me when I asked her what precipitated our family's move from Brooklyn, New York, to her childhood home in Kingston, Jamaica. I was 10 years old, and our move inserted me into a social system I found completely foreign. I arrived in the country to complete 6th grade and sit the Common Entrance Exam, the national exam given at that time to children to determine in which high school they would continue their secondary education. I wanted to fit in, to be like everyone else, and the lens with which I had to make sense of it all was school.

This initial year of my schooling in Jamaica, and the years of high school that followed, offer an interesting set of perspectives in this larger conversation around culture. As a newcomer to the country, my goal was to assimilate, and to do so as quickly as possible. I worked diligently to adopt the accent of my family and classmates, and paid careful attention to the social norms I knew soon had to become my own. When I was a student in the New York City public school system, I was Jamaican and I was American—I was somewhat unique. In Kingston, Jamaica, I was just another Jamaican schoolgirl.

The image of myself that I offered my peers, and the teachers who taught me, was as authentically Jamaican as I could conjure. As far as my teachers could see, I looked like most of the girls in my classes and I sounded like them. Yes, some girls, probably the descendents of Indian, Chinese, and Middle Eastern immigrants to the island (Sherlock & Bennett, 1998), did look different. But we all shared a certain cultural homogeneity rooted in a way of speaking, referring to the events of our lives, and interacting.

For the teachers who taught me, my "Jamaican-ness" was a tangible cultural signpost. For example, my teachers did not know about my being American, as I engaged in a kind of "code-switching"—turning my Jamaican accent on and off depending on with whom I was speaking. There was so much of my background, my "self," that I did not readily reveal to them. If they relied on some cultural aspect of who I was to connect with me personally, to reach me academically, they were somewhat misguided. As I discuss in the remainder of this section, our students are so culturally complex, so much more than we are able to see and perceive, and their educational experiences are shaped by their unique realities.

My somewhat uncommon experience working with deaf and hard of hearing students prompts me to question whether gaining a racial and cultural understanding of one's students holds the key to unlocking the mysteries of how individual students learn. Having racial and cultural competence in the context of being an educator working with deaf and hard of hearing students is a complicated notion.

## Lessons from a Deaf and
## Hard of Hearing Classroom in New York City

*A Look at Deaf Culture.* My inclination is to describe many of the students I taught during these years in terms that define them *first* as being Deaf, and *then* in ways that acknowledge their different races and ethnicities. The journey of trying to articulate my understandings of who my students were as individuals remains complicated. I recognize that these understandings are shaped by both who they were and who I perceived them to be.

A discussion of Deaf culture here is significant. I consciously use a capital "D" in Deaf to acknowledge the existence of a cultural community to which many of my students belonged, as opposed to a lower case "d," which refers to the audiological condition of deafness (Padden & Humphries, 1988). Deaf people historically have rejected the "disability" label (Padden & Humphries, 1988), although it has afforded deaf members of society increased access to education and basic civil rights. In spite of some benefits, many in the community perceive the designation as a challenge to a full appreciation of Deaf culture and its unique language (Lane, Hoffmeister, & Bahan, 1996). In the Deaf community, many of its members do not view deafness as a disability but rather as a cultural difference. Lane (2005) asserts that an appreciation of Deaf people as a unique ethnic group reflects a more enlightened perspective that differs from the "unsuitable construction of the Deaf-World as a disability group" (p. 291).

The Deaf community in America is joined by a common language, American Sign Language—many use it as a primary language—and by the subscription to a set of beliefs about who they are in relation to the larger society (Padden & Humphries, 1988). Membership in this community is not defined solely by an individual's inability to hear (Lane et al., 1996; Moores, 1996). Deaf, hard of hearing, and hearing people are all present in the Deaf community, linked to the Deaf world in various ways. Some of these avenues include the use of American Sign Language, relationships with schools for the deaf, connections to Deaf social and political groups, and, of course, familial bonds (Lane et al., 1996). My work with deaf teenagers gave me access to this community.

The diversity of the Deaf community often was reflected among the students with whom I worked over the years. My students were primarily adolescents of color, and frequently new immigrants or the children of new immigrants. Through my class sessions with them, I learned that some of them were born here in the United States, while others came to this country as young children. They self-identified as Bajan, Bangladeshi, Italian, Jamaican, Mexican, and Puerto Rican, among other nationalities and ethnicities, and often labeled their backgrounds as a mixture of several countries. I mention their backgrounds to illustrate the intricate layers that come together to make each student unique, and to demonstrate that with multiple "cultures," teachers cannot simply pick and choose the facet of a student with which to connect.

In further reflecting upon how these students may have thought of themselves as cultural beings, I recall how surprised I was when I learned which students referred to themselves as deaf, and which preferred the "hard of hearing" designation. These labels taken by the students were not necessarily aligned with the results of their individual audiograms, and also were not predictive of their level of identification as members of the Deaf community. Although I do not explore this topic fully, there is an interesting analogy between how my students chose to identify themselves in terms of deafness, and the choices students make in identifying themselves in terms of race and skin color.

So, I knew that my students were deaf and hard of hearing and were predominantly students of color, but what did this mean? We agree with the research that points to the potential harm that may come from ignoring the race, ethnicity, beliefs, and values of the students in one's classroom (Irvine, 2003). Even if one argues that lack of racial and cultural competence does not actively cause our children harm, one could still concede that inadequate racial and cultural awareness translates into pedagogical experiences that are not as rich and full as they could be or should be.

But will a greater sense of race and culture translate into better teaching? Is it enough to just have this racial and cultural competence? Delpit (1995) cautions that knowledge of race and culture is but one device educators may use in reaching diverse youth. My classroom experience presented the challenge as much more far-reaching than the confines of race and culture.

*Culture in the Classroom.* In my classes I tried to create a community that was self-reflective. We talked often about Deaf culture, other cultures, and culture in general. Research has pointed to the diversity of deaf identities (Parasnis, 1996) and the differing degrees of affiliation with the Deaf community that deaf people express (Bat-Chava, 2000). As lesson material guided what we talked about and the stories we shared, I encountered different voices: students who would say they were "Deaf and proud"; students who expressed feelings of being disabled and limited by their inability to hear, or hear enough; and students who did not articulate an allegiance or even an inclination to any one way of identifying themselves.

There was also real variation in the ways the students chose to communicate. Some talked using their voices, many preferred American Sign Language, and some used a kind of manual signing that sometimes followed English sentence word order and sometimes adhered to the rules and grammar of American Sign Language. Many of the students used some combination of these communication styles and changed and altered styles as they saw fit. My students' use of these communication styles, and the facility with which they combined and altered them, reminded me of my own cultural code-switching.

I tried to think deeply about the ways in which I communicated with my students, sometimes using American Sign Language, sometimes using a kind of signed English, sometimes speaking with my voice, and yet other times using some combination of the above. In choosing how to communicate, I always tried to think about what modality would be most effective in communicating with the student with whom I interacted. Ramsey (2004) writes, "The language socialization, language use, and instructional discourse patterns of Deaf people are critical places to look for ways to make contact with deaf students and help them learn" (p. 56).

Deafness, to a large degree, defined the classroom space that I created with my students. It was not a sufficient lens with which to view my students, however, and I believe the same can be said of teachers who may try to design classroom environments defined by the desire to be multicultural. As a teacher, my work was shaped by my students' inability to hear. The desks in my classroom were arranged in a semicircle, allowing each student to see others' signing. I took opportunities to infuse the classes I taught in U.S. history and government and American Sign Language with references to deaf people and events that provided a way for us to think historically about issues of diversity, as well as discrimination and social justice.

As an educator, I regarded it as my professional charge to try to know more about my students—what interested them, what they knew, and how they learned. I tried to listen to what students told me about their lives outside of the classroom, as this provided one way that I potentially could grow in my understanding of how to teach them. Figuring out what interested my students, as well as what they found challenging, helped me plan creatively and sensitively and to consider ways of piquing their individual interests.

I was definitely more attuned to what worked for some students in some circumstances, but I could not say that I knew what resonated for them beyond the moments where they seemed to connect with the material. Even when I felt like I knew them personally, I realized that I did not know how my students learned.

For many deaf and hard of hearing students, reading and writing pose tremendous difficulties, and there remains a significant achievement gap between deaf and hard of hearing students and their hearing counterparts (King & Quigley, 1985). My challenge was to discover who the students in my classroom were as readers and writers, as learners. I wanted to know who they were as lovers of music and dance, thespians, sisters and brothers, friends, people with individual goals and dreams, as cultural beings. This is an extremely complex endeavor, and I had to do away with the notion that I would ever truly grasp the fullness of who they were. The engine that drives one's pedagogy should be an interest in wanting to always learn more.

Irvine (2003) writes, "Culture is not static, deterministic, or predictive" (p. 7). My students' interests were sometimes different from week to week, or month to month. I could not always predict what lessons would resonate with them, and it was never enough to assume that being attuned and responsive to some facet of their culture or their racial background would be enough to hook them. I easily could have assumed that the understandings I built around Deaf culture would be sufficient cultural awareness for me to have. This was not the case.

***Teaching to Culture.*** I remember teaching several lessons around the "Deaf President Now" protests at Gallaudet University in 1988 that pressured the university's board of trustees to hire its first deaf president. I was confident that students would be captivated by the historical impact of the event and feel empowered by the story of deaf college students having a say in decisions that affected their lives. The actions of these college students ultimately enlightened much of the nation to the desires of deaf people to be treated as equal members of society.

The nation, through the intense media coverage, got to see deaf people who wanted to have agency in their lives and who were proud of their unique Deaf culture (Lane et al., 1996).

However, my students had mixed reactions to the Deaf President Now lessons. Some expressed a real connection to the actions of the deaf student protesters and saw how the group's efforts affected their own lives as deaf members of society. Learning about the protests did not resonate as meaningfully for others, however. I believe some of the students struggled to see their connection to the activist students, who were older, predominantly White, and attending college. While some of my students felt themselves capable of gaining entry into college, several did not see moving on to a university as a realistic opportunity, given their struggles to read and write proficiently.

From the experience of teaching around a topic that I originally presumed to be so relevant to my students' experience but later came to understand as less relevant for some of my students, I learned that attempting to use some aspect of students' culture to define one's work in the classroom is simply not enough. Not only were my groups of students complex and varied, but they were constantly growing and changing as individuals and as learners. Knowledge of Deaf culture informed my teaching of this special population, but my students were not just deaf or hard of hearing or members of Deaf culture, any more than they were just Black, just Dominican, or just from the Bronx. Each student was so much more than any of these.

Gaining cultural competence, if defined as an awareness of Deaf culture in this instance, was important in my work with my deaf and hard of hearing students. Understanding that American Sign Language, or some form of signed language, was an integral piece of their culture and one that had implications for their learning was crucial. I cannot emphasize enough, however, that every child was an individual, and my knowledge of "deafness" was not sufficient to ensure that I would engage them personally or academically.

## PEDRO: TOWARD A PHENOMENOLOGY OF INNER-CITY YOUTH

Like Tarika, I also have been a teacher in urban schools. Most of my experiences have been with students who have been written off as incorrigible and unteachable. From my experience teaching inner-city youth, I have learned that by taking time to listen without judgment, one can begin to understand that there are legitimate reasons for the anger they so often exhibit, an anger that frequently contributes to bad choices and behavior that is self-destructive and injurious to the communities where they live. For me, understanding the source of their anger is not the same as justifying or condoning how that anger may be manifest or expressed. However, without an understanding of its source, it may be impossible to figure out how to help young people to channel feelings of anger and alienation in more positive and constructive ways, or how to intervene so that some of the more destructive tendencies among inner-city youth can be prevented. I also have come to understand that there is logic behind the choices they make, one that grows out of a sensibility and sometimes even a critical awareness of the forces stacked against them in American society and in their local environment. Like Freire's (1970) search for the "generative themes" (p. 36) in the lives of adult learners (the words, ideas, and phrases that capture the passions and sensibilities of a particular community or group), I have come to see that understanding the logic that guides the behavior of inner-city youth is the first step to engaging young people in an educational process aimed at changing the way they respond to the forms of hardship and the forces of oppression that shape and constrain their lives.

## Countering the Drug Culture and Amoral Capitalism

I gained this understanding working in inner-city communities in the Bay Area. From 1986 to 1988 I was employed as the Executive Assistant to the Mayor of Berkeley, California. In this role, I had primary responsibility for helping the Mayor figure out how best to respond to problems such as homelessness, drug trafficking, and urban blight. Initially, I embraced my work with enthusiasm and zeal because I believed that I was in a position where I could play a role in developing social policy and truly make a difference. However, after a few months on the job I began to realize that rather than being in a position where I could solve problems, I was merely in a position where I would have to explain to the community why their city government was so ineffective. Much of our failure could be explained by the fact that we lacked the resources to address the roots of problems like homelessness and drug trafficking. I soon realized that when I was asked to address an irate group of residents who wanted to know why the police were unable to prevent drive-by shootings or drug dealing that was occurring openly on street corners, explaining the inadequacy of city government was unlikely to appease them.

Frustrated with my job, I began seeking out opportunities to work with young people in schools, hoping that education could serve as a means of preventing some of the problems I was grappling with in city government. I sought out other adults who shared my concern about what was happening to young people in our community, and helped to establish new organizations that could attempt to respond.[1] On one occasion I was asked by a middle school principal to speak to a group of boys who were considered "at risk" due to their poor grades and disruptive behavior. She asked if I would meet with the boys on a regular basis and serve as a mentor. I agreed, hoping that in this new role I would be far more effective at addressing some of the social problems I was being asked to respond to in the Mayor's office. However, I soon realized that working with this group of boys would be more challenging than I had expected. At my first meeting with the group, I discovered that all 12 were involved, either directly or indirectly, with selling drugs. The boys were the ones who brought the topic up when I asked what they were interested in. They laughed and shouted, "balling," "hustlin'," and "slanging rock"—all street terms used for drug dealing.

Initially, I tried unsuccessfully to engage them in a debate about the ethics of drug dealing, hoping that I might convince them that selling drugs was wrong. I spoke about the great harm that was being inflicted on abusers and their families. I brought up the violence drug dealing generated due to the competition among dealers for control of territory. However, all of the arguments I made failed completely. As I listened to these young men laugh and joke about their experiences selling drugs, I realized that they too had an addiction, an addiction to drug dealing and the money it generated for them. I knew too that their unwillingness to "just say no" was rooted in their embrace of the logic of rugged individualism and amoral, predatory capitalism. Drug dealing was a business, they argued, and given that all of them were poor and needed money to support themselves and in some cases their families, from their point of view selling drugs made sense. As one young man put it bluntly, "What's a nigga to do?"

To counter their logic, or at least find a way to undermine it, I decided to change the topic. I began asking them questions about their lives outside of school in the hope that by learning more about them I might find a way to engage them in a critical discussion about what they were doing. I soon began to learn about their families, and as I asked the boys to talk about their role within their families, I learned that none of them lived with their fathers (a few admitted not knowing who their fathers were) and that several were responsible for the care of younger siblings. This insight about the roles they played in their families gave me an opening that I thought I could use to return to our conversation about drugs. After one student described how he had to drop off his younger sister at school each morning and pick her up in the afternoon, I asked the young man, "Would you sell drugs to your sister?" He looked at me with shock and disbelief. "No way. Drugs are poison." I then turned to one of the other boys in the group and asked him, "What about you? Would you sell drugs to his sister?" The boy paused to think for a moment and then responded, "Yes. I'd do it because it's a business, and if I didn't sell to her someone else would." I then asked the first boy how he felt about the fact that someone he called a friend said he would sell drugs to his little sister. The boy responded, "That's wrong. He's supposed to be my boy." The other boy then said, "I'm not saying I will sell drugs to your sister. I'm saying that if she asked me I would. At least I could make sure she got some good drugs."

With that admission, the ethical discussion that I had hoped to initiate about drug dealing and social responsibility ensued. For the first time issues related to social responsibility and the impact of drug dealing and drug use in Black communities could be raised and debated. Several of the boys admitted how disturbed they were at seeing adults they knew—relatives, neighbors, and friends—become addicted to drugs. Although there was laughter and ridicule expressed about "tweakers" and "base heads" (slang terms used to describe crack abusers), "chicken heads" and "crack hoes" (terms used to describe women who exchange sex for drugs), for the first time the young men acknowledged that crack cocaine was having a devastating impact on their community. Interestingly, once we got beyond the bravado of drug dealing and they acknowledged the impact that crack use was having on their community and their lives, they were less willing to brag about their involvement in the drug trade and more willing to admit that what they were doing was wrong.

## The Importance of Learning from Our Students

Over the years I have found that engaging inner-city youth in a critical analysis of their lives and the forces that shape and constrain them and their communities must begin from an awareness of what their lives are like and how they have come to perceive and interpret their social reality. In order to gain this understanding, educators must be willing to open themselves to learning about the lives of the students they teach. It is important to recognize that such pedagogical practice must include: (1) an openness to hearing young people share their perceptions of the social reality they inhabit, and (2) a willingness to engage in acts of solidarity in the fight against the oppression they face.

For me, this is more than an academic exercise. The conditions facing many inner-city youth are extreme—homicide rates remain high (in cities like Oakland, Detroit, Baltimore, and Washington, DC they are rising) and incarceration rates for juveniles show no signs of being reduced in the near future (Krisberg, Marchianna, & Baird, 2007). Given the dire circumstances confronting inner-city youth, I have found it helpful to draw upon the ideas of Paulo Freire (1970) for a "theory of change" that can guide the work of teaching those students. There is a crisis facing inner-city youth in the United States, and it is essential that those who would like to do something to address this crisis recognize that no solutions are possible unless young people are active participants in designing and implementing them.

## THOUGHTS FOR TEACHERS

So, with educators potentially understanding the value of celebrating diversity, or moving away from what King (1991) calls "dysconscious racism" characterized by "limited and distorted understandings" (pp. 133–134) about inequity and cultural diversity, what do teachers do now?

Sleeter (2000) writes, "Many young people show great interest when issues they recognize as real, challenging, and ethical are opened up in the classroom" (p. 2). During our time in schools, we can affirm that the most meaningful exchanges we have had with students were rooted in honest conversations. These conversations were not always about what they were learning in school; often, they allowed students to share insights informed as much by who they were as students as who they were out of school.

We are all teachers of diverse students and must capitalize on the power we have to make language and culture transparent and talked about.

Fecho (2004) writes about students being able to explore, "interrogating self and others" (p. 126). He believes this is how students come to a richer understanding of themselves as learners. Taken together, the beliefs, ideas, and attitudes of the educators he has studied form a powerful vision for teaching that can inspire every teacher to embrace the complexity inherent in teaching, and push teachers to test the limits of their understandings of their students.

Although Bain (2004) focuses on what the best teachers at the college level do in their work with students, his ideas are salient for all educators. He emphasizes the influence of teachers' general attitudes, their faith in their students, their willingness to have students express agency in their educational decisions, and the fostering of relationships based on a commitment to shared learning goals and mutual respect.

The ideas we have shared are not new ones. Instead, they are insights we suspect many in the field have had and may or may not have shared with their colleagues. In writing this chapter, we are making some of our private understandings more public in the hope that they will resonate for others who are trying to make sense of their efforts to teach in a way that values students' *many* individual cultures.

As teachers, we are all called upon to think deeply about how our own thinking and attitudes, along with those of our students, come together to shape our individual classroom communities. Our most marginalized students most need teachers who commit to knowing them fully.

## NOTES

Photo of Tarika Barrett by Michael H. O'Loughlin.

1. One of the organizations that I helped to create in 1987 was Black Men United for Change. My thinking was that by bringing concerned Black men together to address the plight of at-risk Black youth, we might have greater ability to respond to the problems. Today, similar organizations exist throughout the United States, most operating under the name 100 Black Men.

## REFERENCES

Bain, K. (2004). *What the best college teachers do*. Cambridge, MA: Harvard University Press.

Bat-Chava, Y. (2000). Diversity of deaf identities. *American Annals of the Deaf, 145*(5), 420–428.

Delpit, L. D. (2006). *Other people's children: Cultural conflict in the classroom.* New York: New Press. (Original work published 1995)

Fecho, B. (2004). *"Is this English?": Race, language, and culture in the classroom.* New York: Teachers College Press.

Freire, P. (1970). *The pedagogy of the oppressed.* New York: Continuum.

Gay, G. (2000). *Culturally responsive teaching: Theory, research, and practice.* New York: Teachers College Press.

Irvine, J. J. (2003). *Educating teachers for diversity: Seeing with a cultural eye.* New York: Teachers College Press.

King, C. M., & Quigley, S. P. (1985). *Reading and deafness.* San Diego, CA: College-Hill Press.

King, J. E. (1991). Dysconscious racism: Ideology, identity, and the miseducation of teachers. *Journal of Negro Education, 60*(2), 133–146.

Krisberg, B., Marchianna, S., & Baird, C. (2007). *Continuing the struggle for justice: 100 years of the National Council on Crime and Delinquency.* Thousand Oaks, CA: Sage.

Lane, H. (2005). Ethnicity, ethics, and the deaf-world. *Journal of Deaf Studies and Deaf Education, 10*(3), 291–320.

Lane, H. L., Hoffmeister, R., & Bahan, B. J. (1996). *A journey into the deaf-world.* San Diego, CA: DawnSignPress.

Lipman, P. (1995). "Bringing out the best in them": The contribution of culturally relevant teachers to education. *Theory into Practice, 34*(3), 203–208.

Moores, D. F. (1996). *Educating the deaf: Psychology, principles, and practices* (4th ed.). Boston: Houghton Mifflin.

Padden, C., & Humphries. T. (1988). *Deaf in America: Voices from a culture.* Cambridge, MA: Harvard University Press.

Parasnis, I. (1996). On interpreting the deaf experience within the context of cultural and language diversity. In I. Parasnis (Ed.), *Cultural and language diversity and the deaf experience* (pp. 3–19). Cambridge & New York: Cambridge University Press.

Ramsey, C. (2004). What does culture have to do with the education of students who are deaf or hard of hearing? In B. J. Brueggemann (Ed.), *Literacy and deaf people: Cultural and contextual perspectives* (pp. 47–58). Washington, DC: Gallaudet University Press.

Sherlock, P M., & Bennett, H. (1998). *The story of the Jamaican people.* Kingston, Jamaica: Ian Randle Publishers.

Sleeter, C. E. (2000). Creating an empowering multicultural curriculum. *Race, Gender & Class in Education, 7*(3), 178. 1. Retrieved February 3, 2006, from Alt-Press Watch database (Document ID: 494618041)

Sleeter, C. E. (2001). Preparing teachers for culturally diverse schools: Research and the overwhelming presence of whiteness. *Journal of Teacher Education, 52*(2), 94–106.

# CHAPTER NINE

# Visions of Teachers Leaving No More Children Behind

*Jeffrey M. R. Duncan-Andrade*

## A PERSONAL ANECDOTE

In 1989, I was admitted as an undergraduate to the University of California at Berkeley. After my admission, the university sent me a request for "evidence" that "proved" I am of Mexican descent. They wanted to count me in their non-White racial admissions statistics. At first, I thought I would just send them my birth certificate. However, as is the case with most Chicanos, my birth certificate classifies me as Caucasian. In my case, this is probably the result of two things. First, I am racially mixed—my mother is Méxicana and my father is White (Scottish). Second, babies of Mexican origin (and other South and Latin American origins) historically have been classified as Caucasian. Even today, birth certificates and the Census do not recognize Mexican as a race. My mother was pained and insulted by this request. Ultimately, she reluctantly wrote a letter describing my "olive colored skin, dark hair, and dark eyes," and her family's immigration from México.

This was the first time my family explicitly discussed the significance of race, even though it was constantly present. My abuelita lived with us and helped raise me, my three brothers, and my three sisters. Traditional Mexican foods were standard fare, and Spanish was the language of choice when Mom's family called or when we visited them in México. As a child, I was proud to be Mexican, but I never felt like there was a place to express that pride in school or the larger society. Peers' snide remarks and messages from the mainstream suggested I should be ashamed of being Mexican and a "half-breed." But none of these deprecating dialogues (real and hidden) were coming out of my home.

At home, we were a big family with our own culture and enough of our own problems. We were busy trying to figure out the sum of our parts: seven half-breed children, one devout Catholic abuelita, one second-generation equally devout Catholic Méxicana mother, and one converted-to-Catholic Marine Corps father who flew his Scottish family crest in his workroom. My family is the embodiment of the complicated beautiful mess that represents the way we talk about race in this country. My family, like most, would create tremendous difficulties for any anthropologist attempting to reduce and essentialize people's behaviors based on their race. But we do not live inside our families all the time. The broader society finds it much easier to deal with the complicated humanity of ethnicity, language, and culture when it can be reduced to a box—what are you? I will always be the son of both my mother and father. But on the day that U.C. Berkeley made my mother write that letter, the broader society was permitted to classify me as something beyond just being my parents' son.

## RACE IS A SOCIAL PARADOX

Cornel West is quite right in his book title, *Race Matters* (1993). As a society, we have created a conundrum around race that I see no easy way around. The concept of race is a social paradox; it is a socially bankrupt concept used to divide and conquer people of color, but it is also an opportunity for connecting people to their shared experiences with racism as people of color. It is difficult for me to fully wrap my head around a strategy whereby a socially engineered concept designed to divide people will ever provide the pathway to peace and justice for the world. To the degree that we attempt to develop our identities based solely on racial constructs, I am convinced that we will remain a society divided and that ultimately we will destroy ourselves; at present, we appear to be moving full steam ahead in that direction.

We are not too far down this path of racial divisiveness to correct our course. This does not mean that we should be pursuing a color-blind society. On the contrary, we should celebrate our multiracial society. This celebration should begin with an honest and public admission that we have always been, and currently remain, a racist society. Once we find the courage to recognize that, we can spend the next several centuries earnestly undoing the racist society we built. This, of course, also will mean putting an immediate stop to our racist exploitation of non-White people in other nations.

If we can meet the challenge of equity and justice for all people, we will have met any society's greatest and only truly meaningful challenge. As it stands, our nation does not display the capacity to celebrate our cultural richness. We have not even found it in ourselves to look in the mirror and admit that our country was founded on genocide, built by slave labor, and sustained by racial exploitation to this day.

In the wake of Hurricane Katrina, the nation's apartheid-like social structure once again has been brutally exposed. Schools, specifically educators, must make room for students to engage in critical conversation about the social forces that create such apartheid and suffering for people of color. To meet this challenge, educators must be prepared and supported to implement a curriculum and pedagogy that deliberately confront structures of racism and humanize students. These educators will develop connections between students by engaging them in critical analyses of how racist structures of inequality work, and by facilitating understandings of their relationship to one another as people who have endured the suffering caused by racism. Ultimately, effective educators will be able to teach the concept of race as a social paradox. These discussions will help students learn to identify with the suffering of other students in the class and around the globe.

It will take a national commitment to these kinds of teaching principles if schools aim to prepare a citizenry that will topple racism, White supremacy, and the colonialist mentality that dominates virtually every major social structure in this nation. When we have met this challenge with our children, they will build the society we heretofore have lacked the courage to create. In that society, mothers will never suffer the insult of having to describe their child's phenotypical features and immigration status so that an institution can count and calibrate its data. In that society, all people will have access and we will celebrate them all.

All students should have access to teachers who can develop these kinds of classroom cultures. However, particular attention should be paid to the development of these skills in urban teachers because of the persistent low-quality instruction that takes place there. Numerous studies have documented this urban educational inequality, helping to pressure elected officials into creating policies such as the 2001 No Child Left Behind (NCLB) Act. Sadly, NCLB has become another example of the unfulfilled promise that the public can and should expect every classroom to be staffed by a "highly qualified teacher." Such an expectation is currently unattainable because of three major shortcomings in our dialogues about effective educators: (1) we have not clearly defined the core indicators of a highly qualified teacher; (2) we have not clearly established the significance of the urban social context for this definition; and (3) we have failed to develop effective professional supports, school cultures, preservice training, and educational policies that reflect knowledge of effective pedagogy in urban contexts. These shortcomings offer a challenge and an opportunity for educational researchers to answer long-standing questions about effective teaching. That is, how is it possible that a few teachers are successful in schools where most are failing to reach their students? What are the identifiable strategies and conditions that make these teachers more highly qualified than their counterparts? How can other teachers learn from these successes to develop similarly effective practices?

## TEACHERS USING
## SOCIAL JUSTICE PEDAGOGY IN URBAN SCHOOLS

In an effort to begin answering these questions, this chapter discusses the work of four teachers (two high school and two elementary teachers) in South Central Los Angeles. They each participated in a 3-year study of social justice pedagogy in urban schools. These four distinguished themselves as exceptional urban educators in all the ways we might measure excellent teaching. They were definitely racially and culturally competent. Their students were high achievers by traditional standards (test scores, grades, college attendance). Students were also high achievers by the standards of critical pedagogy (critique of structural inequality and oppression, critical reading of the word and their world, individual and collective agency for social change).

### The Teachers

*Steven Lapu.* Lapu was kicked out of the Los Angeles public schools when he was in high school (pseudonyms are used for all participants). A Filipino man, he grew up active in gang life and experienced many of the social and economic challenges that confront his students. After several years as a teacher's aide in urban elementary schools in Los

Angeles, he found a program for ex-gang members that allowed him to enroll as an undergraduate student at California State University, Los Angeles, which ultimately led him to pursue his teaching credential. He had been teaching for 6 years at Crenshaw High School in South Central Los Angeles when this study began.

*Lisa Cross.* Lisa grew up in an upper-middle-class family on the East Coast. A White woman from a well-educated family, Lisa had the benefit of a first-rate education and is a graduate of Columbia University. She came to Los Angeles with the intention of using her privilege to disrupt racial and social inequality in the educational system. She had been teaching for 4 years as a high school English teacher in Lynwood (a city bordering Watts and Compton in South Central Los Angeles).

*Erika Truth.* Erika spent much of her childhood in East Palo Alto (EPA), California. During her time there, EPA was reputed to be the murder capital of the country. A Black woman, Erika found her way into the classroom because of her commitment to social change in Black and Latino communities. A single mother of a son who attended the school where she taught, she was acutely aware of the challenges facing children and parents in urban schools. She had been teaching for 9 years, and was a 4th-grade teacher in Watts (South Central Los Angeles).

*Andre Veracruz.* Andre grew up on the urban fringe of San Diego, attending schools that were heavily populated by recent Mexican immigrants, Filipinos, and Chicanos. The son of Filipino immigrants, Andre is the middle child of three. He was a successful student but as a young person often found himself on the margins because he was heavily involved in graffiti art. His ongoing love of "graf-art" and hip-hop were points of common interest with many of his students, and frequently endeared him to some of his most marginalized students. Andre had been teaching for 5 years as a 5th-grade teacher in Watts.

## CORE PILLARS OF RACIAL AND CULTURAL COMPETENCE

The classroom practice of each of these teachers was unique to his or her personality, but in all of the classes, I consistently witnessed five principles of pedagogy that are the focus of this chapter. I explain these principles as core pillars of racial and cultural competence. What follows is a description of each of these pillars and an explanation of its significance to the teacher's effectiveness with students.

## Pillar #1: Critically Conscious Purpose

The first question I usually ask teachers I am working with is, "Why do you teach?" Most teachers respond in one of two ways: (1) I teach because I love kids, or (2) I teach because I want to be part of the solution, not part of the problem. In separate interviews, these four teachers all responded to this question differently than most other teachers, yet their answers were remarkably similar to one another. They said that they teach because they believe their students, specifically low-income children of color, are the group most likely to change the world. They explained this belief by saying that the children most disenfranchised from society are the ones with the least to lose, and thus are the most likely to be willing to take the risks necessary to change society. This belief that they are teaching young people destined to change the world is vital to the level of seriousness with which they approach their jobs.

I call this a critically conscious purpose because their perspectives were not guided by some romantic vision of changing the world. Instead, they recognized that the students most likely to change the world were also the ones most likely to struggle in a typical classroom environment. They would not be the favorite students, but the bane of the teacher's existence; the agent of change would not be prone to follow the rules, but rather to test boundaries. To prepare fertile ground for all their students to succeed, particularly the students who would be risk takers, these teachers worked at understanding the history of the communities where they worked and the people who lived there. They had studied, and several had lived under, various forms of oppression that helped them formulate critical awareness and analyses of structural and material inequities.

One example of their sense of purpose, evident across their practices, was the pedagogical strategy of redefining success for their students. They talked to students about using school as a way to return to their communities, rather than as a strategy for escaping them. They developed curriculum that reflected this possibility. This strategy led to improved learning outcomes measured by traditional means (increased test scores and grades). It also led to student work (writing, presentations, projects) that reflected critical thinking and a sense of hope and purpose that they could be critical agents of change in their communities.

In Mr. Veracruz's 5th-grade class in Watts, he was mandated to use Open Court, a scripted literacy program. Many teachers feel trapped by scripted programs, arguing that they stifle their ability to be creative with curriculum. Mr. Veracruz was critical of scripted programs, but felt that too many of his colleagues used them as an excuse to stop planning their lessons creatively. He said:

> Scripted programs are a problem and they should be eliminated, but they are here and I'm tired of hearing teachers use them as an excuse for being uncreative in their lesson planning. Scripted programs are like anything else in this culture of testing; they are either a crutch for not teaching or they are a set of rules and guidelines that you can manipulate. I don't really have a problem with the key concepts that the scripted curriculum tells me to teach, just like I don't really have a problem with most of the standards I'm supposed to teach. The problem comes when you stop coming up with ways to make those things relevant to kids' lives.

Mr. Veracruz's approach to scripted programs reflected his critically conscious purpose for teaching. He expected his students to be able to read and write as well as any student in the country, but he recognized that scripted programs like Open Court often are not designed to reflect the lived experiences of low-income students of color. His response was to remake the assignments so that they taught the same literacy standards while using activities that reflected the lives and needs of his students.

### Pillar #2: Duty

The second trait I saw across the practices of these teachers was a distinctive sense of duty to students and the community. The sense of duty among these teachers reflected Carter G. Woodson's (1933/1990) distinction between persons who fashion themselves as leaders and persons who perceive themselves as responsible for serving the community. Woodson wrote:

> You cannot serve people by giving them orders as to what to do. The real servant of the people must live among them, think with them, feel for them, and die for them. . . . The servant of the people, unlike the leader, is not on a high horse trying to carry the people to some designated point to which he would like to go for his own advantage. The servant of the people is down among them, living as they live, doing what they do and enjoying what they enjoy. He may be a little better informed than some of the other members of the group; it may be that he has had some experience they have not had, but in spite of this advantage he should have more humility than those whom he serves. (p. 131)

Similar to Woodson's "servant of the people," these teachers had a level of commitment to their teaching that reflected the fact that they saw themselves as members of the communities where they taught. This often led them to invest in those students that many other teachers had already written off as hopeless; instead, they saw those students as members of their community whom they could not simply disregard.

All of these teachers were committed to a consistent presence in the school community and in the lives of the students and their families. They made deliberate efforts to stay late in the community on school nights, to attend community events on weekends and in the summers, to know where their students lived, and to know the parents of their students. They described their decision to become members of the communities where they taught as part of a commitment to solidarity with their students, as opposed to empathy. In so doing, they reflected a sense of duty compatible with Woodson's argument that to truly serve people one must remain connected to them and humble among them.

### Pillar #3: Preparation

The four teachers discussed here were always at, or near, the top of their schools in traditional measures of student success, despite having (and many times accepting in mid-year) students whom colleagues had forced out of their classrooms. Even though these achievement patterns suggest they were already excellent pedagogues, each of these teachers spent a tremendous amount of time preparing for classes. I mention this because of the not uncommon notion that good teachers have their curriculum and classroom management mastered and thus can operate on autopilot. These teachers dispelled that myth. They constantly prepared for their practice. Their intense commitment to preparation gave them expectations of success that are rare in schools where achievement is so low. The time they spent preparing their lessons and units fostered a contagious level of excitement, passion, and belief in the curriculum when they delivered it to students.

When I asked them about the amount of time they spent preparing for their teaching, none of them could quantify it. They commented on the fact that they could not really identify a time when they were not preparing for their teaching in some way or another. They each recounted stories about stumbling upon a film, book, artifact, or teaching technique that they collected for later use, even during time they had marked out as "time away from teaching." This constant preparation to improve their practice harkens back to their comments about their sense of duty to the profession: "Teacher is who I am, not what I do."

After spending 3 years with these teachers, I came to realize that there was virtually no part of their teaching that was not subject to revision or total discard. Regardless of whether they were teaching the same grade or subject the next year, they would rethink curriculum units from top to bottom before reteaching them. In addition, they constantly sought professional development opportunities to expand their knowledge, particularly in areas where they felt they were lacking, and regularly solicited new pedagogical tools from colleagues.

### Pillar #4: Socratic Sensibility

Socrates often is credited with having said that the wise person knows that he or she knows nothing. What he meant, of course, is that the wise person recognizes that he or she always has more to learn. Cornel West (2001) has argued for the development of this lifelong commitment to learning through the development of what he calls a "Socratic sensibility." West describes the person with this sensibility as someone who understands both Socrates' statement that "the unexamined life is not worth living" (Plato, 1966, p. 38) and Malcolm X's statement that the "examined life is painful" (West, 2001).

The teachers in this study lived out this Socratic sensibility by striking a delicate balance between confidence in their ability as teachers and frequent self-critique. They constantly reflected on their daily practice and their relationships with students in an effort to get a little better each day. To aid in this process, they encouraged all types of visitors (parents, teachers, future teachers, and university professors) to their classrooms. They were particularly open to those who were willing to give them critical feedback about their practice. However, it is important to note that this self-critique did not come across as self-doubt. As Mr. Veracruz put it, "Most of the criticisms I get from observers in my class are critiques I have already made of myself. So, I welcome that reminder that although I'm good at what I do, I need to get better. That is what keeps me on top of my game."

This self-analysis came about, in large part, due to their Socratic sensibility. They understood the challenge implicit in Socrates' advice that "all great undertakings are risky, and, as they say, what is worth while is always difficult" (Plato, 2003, p. 220). They also understood that to truly embrace the great challenges of teaching in urban schools, they had to face the painful part of the examined life to which Malcolm X referred. That is, they understood their duty to connect their pedagogy to the harsh realities of poor, urban communities. An e-mail to me from Ms. Truth reveals the great undertaking required of educators who aim to respond to the reality of the conditions of urban life, and the pain that sometimes accompanies self-reflection on that response. She wrote:

> Today was an almost unbearably sad day at school . . . according to my students (all of which were SOBBING) two young men (black) were sitting in a car yesterday afternoon . . . some men in a car rolled up, got out and shot one in the eye (his head exploded) there was a 3-month-old in the back seat (she was left "unharmed") the other got out and ran (they call him "baby" Marcus) the guys ran after him and shot him in the back and then more when he fell . . . both men dead, the perpetrators got away . . . the nephew of one is in my class, the brother of the other is in [Mr. Randall's] class. This is a close community so word spread pretty rapidly yesterday. For an hour and a half [this morning] the kids all just talked and cried. I felt ill-equipped to handle a crisis like this but, we got through it. . . . I said as little as possible, I cried with the kids, we all consoled each other, and others began sharing different stories of violence and loss . . . in the end, I did what I thought (and hope) was best . . . tried to empower them with the belief that they must work to become the warriors who combat the senseless violence and madness on the streets. I also gave them some "street lessons": walk against traffic, don't sit in parked cars chillin' with your friends, be vigilant, check your surroundings. We're making cards, and going to send a little

money to the families . . . and the kids all seem to feel a little
better. . . . how would you handle this? It looks as if many
teachers didn't say or do much . . . feeling a bit weary today.

Ms. Truth's class collected over $100 for the family. She delivered the
money, along with several cards expressing their condolences, at the
funeral of one of the murdered young men.

This level of openness between Ms. Truth and her students was
built over time, both through her awareness of conditions in the community, but also through deliberate class structures that allowed students multiple opportunities to share their struggles and pain. In most
urban schools, there is no formal structure to support teachers and prepare them to handle such tragic events. In fact, in many schools teachers are discouraged from participating in students' lives at this level.
The result is, as Ms. Truth mentions, that most teachers avoid or ignore
tragedies that go on in the community—these teachers did not.

## Pillar #5: Trust

The fifth trait I saw while studying these teachers was a distinct
commitment to building trust with their students. The fact that trust
is important in a teacher–student relationship should not be surpris-
ing to anyone. However, it was the unique way that these teachers
talked about trust that struck me. During interviews with me, they
each described trust in the same way as Mr. Lapu, who said:

Many of the teachers I have been around can't understand why
students don't trust them. They think of trust as something that
is automatic for teachers, like students are just going to trust
them because they are in the position of teacher. But, it doesn't
work like that. You have to earn it [trust] every day out here.
Just because you have a bond with a student today doesn't
guarantee that that bond will be there tomorrow if you don't
keep working on it. That's just ahistorical. Let's be real here. I
represent an institution that represents the state that represents
a history of colonialism and repression. Why *would* [emphasis
in speech] students trust me? Every day I have to fight against
that history. Sure I'm mad about that, but it's not the students'
fault and it's not my fault, so I don't take it personally. But I do
recognize that trust is easier to lose than to get.

These teachers understood that government institutions, such as schools, have a negative history in poor and non-White communities. No matter how good their intentions, they were aware that as ambassadors of the institution of school, they were connected to that history. This awareness allowed them to be cognizant of this obstacle for building trust with students and the community, and also helped them to understand the importance of standing in opposition to school policies that were oppressive, racist, and colonialist, and that perpetuated the cycles of inequality.

Evidence of their commitment to earn the trust of their students was clear in every aspect of their teaching, from their curriculum, to their grading, to their classroom management policies, to their pedagogy. However, it is probably best explained through the relationships that they built with their students. As with their sense of duty, their activities were driven by a long-haul commitment to their students and the community, one that did not permit them to give up on a student whose transformation was not as rapid as the teacher might like. Their perspective might best be described using one of Lisa Delpit's (1995/2006) book titles; they saw their students as their children, not "other people's children."

The construction of a classroom culture that fostered trust among the students, and between the teacher and the students, was the result of many nuanced parts of their practice. However, in their own ways, they all demonstrated and articulated a concrete understanding of two key factors that allowed trust to develop. First, they understood the distinction between being liked and being loved by their students. Second, they did not coddle students, particularly those with whom they had built strong relationships. As Ms. Truth explained:

> Many of these teachers are so afraid that students won't like them if they discipline them that they end up letting students do things that they would never permit from their own children. They lower their standards and will take any old excuse from students for why they did not do their homework, or why they cannot sit still in class or do their work. Not me. You gotta work in my class. I can be unrelenting at times, probably even overbearing. Oh, I might give a student slack here or there, but most of the time I'm like, "Go tell it to someone else because I'm not trying to hear that from you right now. We've got work to do."

The line between high expectations and unreasonable demands can be a slippery slope for teachers. But so is the line between people that we love and people that we like. The people that we love can demand levels of commitment from us that defy even our own notions of what we are capable of. People that we like, but do not love, typically are not able to push the limits of our abilities. Nothing more clearly divides these two groups of people in our life than the level of trust we have in them.

In the case of these four teachers, the move from being liked to being loved did not happen because of the demands they made of students. It happened because of the love and support that accompanied those raised expectations. Sometimes this was simple encouragement, but many times it meant amplifying the personal support given to students. This support took many forms: after-school and weekend tutoring, countless meals, rides home, phone/text messaging/e-mail/ instant messaging sessions, and endless prodding, cajoling, and all-around positive harassment. These additional investments of time and money clarified for students that these expectations came with the teacher's recognition that everyone needs help along the way. And when that help is from someone who loves you, in spite of your short-comings, you learn to trust that person.

The development of these trusting relationships also resulted in these teachers being indignant about student failure. This was due largely to the fact that they saw the failure of a student as their own failure. At the same time, they never excused students from their re-sponsibility. This seems to me remarkably similar to the approach suc-cessful parents take with their children, although the teacher–student relationships will never quite measure up to those of strong parent–children bonds.

## IMPLICATIONS

The stories of these teachers are inspiring, but what about achieve-ment? Do these pillars actually increase the academic performance of students? The answer is a resounding "yes." These teachers were at the top of their schools in many of the ways we traditionally measure success (test scores, literacy and mathematics acquisition, grades, at-tendance, graduation, and college enrollment). However, perhaps the most important realization for me was that they reached this achievement because they focused on the humanizing elements of education to which most schools pay little attention.

While NCLB and local educational policy have turned their sights to quantitative measures of achievement, these teachers focused on education as a humanizing project. They recognized that of all the things we debate in education, there is one fact on which we have relative consensus. From child psychology to pedagogical theory to cognitive theory, our most basic understanding of the necessary conditions for learning suggests that positive self-identity, a sense of purpose, and hope are critical prerequisites for achievement. The test score fetish of the high-stakes era has turned us away from prioritizing these measures of effective teaching, even though gains in these areas are the key to raising test scores.

To be sure, it is much easier to develop a test preparation program in a corporate lab than to pinpoint the elements of pedagogy that humanize students. Developing effective urban educators is hard work and it is certainly not as cost-effective as scripted curricula, test prep manuals, and one-day trainings—as long as the students who have always failed under high-stakes testing continue to fail. The correlation between high parental income and success on achievement tests is well documented, as are the seemingly intractable relationships between race and test scores. It seems a plausible conclusion that no small part of those gaps is the result of the fact that most successful students enter school with a positive self-identity, a clear purpose for attending school, and a justifiable hope that school success will be rewarded in the larger society. For most low-income children, particularly low-income children of color, there is little in the history of school or the broader society that would concretely justify any of those three beliefs. There will always be exceptions—that young person who finds cause for hope in the system—but sadly exceptions are all we find today in urban schools.

I am confident that this study could have been done in any successful teacher's classroom, with similar results. I find myself concluding that I have discovered nothing particularly groundbreaking about effective teaching in urban schools. It is hard work and there are no shortcuts. We will never develop some ideal instructional program that can be exported from classroom to classroom. In the end, programs that come out of boxes do not work. Great teaching will always be about relationships, and programs do not build relationships, people do. The truth of the matter is that we have the know-how to make achievement in urban schools the norm, as it is in high-income communities. There are successful teachers in every school, even where failure is rampant. We should be spending more time figuring out who they are and studying what they do and why it works. This research should guide teacher-credentialing programs and school-based professional support structures so that more teachers can develop those effective practices.

When I began this study, I had been an urban classroom teacher for 10 years. At the outset, I was deeply pessimistic about the future of the profession and our ability to meet the challenges confronting us in urban schools. After this study, I am tentatively hopeful. This hope comes from the fact that almost every teacher that I worked with over those 3 years (more than 150 teachers in all) demonstrated most, if not all, of these five pillars. Given the right professional support, the majority of these urban teachers have the potential to develop into exceptional teachers.

This decade will usher in upwards of one million new teachers, mostly in urban schools (National Commission on Teaching and America's Future, 2003). This brings with it an unprecedented opportunity to swing the pendulum toward educational equity. We can, if we so desire, invest heavily in refocusing our efforts to recruit, train, and develop urban educators who will be racially and culturally competent. Studies such as this suggest that we can know what makes effective urban educators. We can name the characteristics of their practices. We can link those characteristics to increases in engagement and achievement. If we fail to significantly invest in the support and development of these characteristics in this new wave of teachers, as we have with their predecessors, we almost certainly will end up as the nation that James Baldwin (1961) foreshadowed over 45 years ago.

> What it comes to, finally, is that the nation has spent a large part of its time and energy looking away from one of the principal facts of its life. . . . Any honest examination of the national life proves how far we are from the standard of human freedom with which we began. . . . If we are not capable of this examination, we may yet become one of the most distinguished and monumental failures in the history of nations. (p. 99)

And if we fail, let us be clear that it will not be for lack of know-how, but for the lack of determination to provide a quality education for all our young people.

# REFERENCES

Baldwin, J. (1961). *Nobody knows my name.* New York: Dell.

Delpit, L. (2006). *Other people's children: Cultural conflict in the classroom.* New York: The New Press. (Original work published 1995)

National Commission on Teaching and America's Future. (2003). *No dream denied: A pledge to America's children* (Summary Report). Washington, DC: Author.

Plato. (1966). *Plato in twelve volumes* (Vol. 1) (H. N. Fowler, Trans.). Cambridge, MA: Harvard University Press.

Plato. (2003). *The republic* (D. Lee, Trans.). London: Penguin Press.

West, C. (1993). *Race matters.* Boston: Beacon.

West, C. (2001). *Progressive politics in these times.* Mario Savio Annual Lecture Series, Berkeley, CA.

Woodson, C. (1990). *Miseducation of the Negro.* Trenton, NJ: Africa World Press. (Original work published 1933)

# CHAPTER TEN

# Going Beyond the Classroom: Activism as Racial and Cultural Competence

## Kitty Kelly Epstein

The United States spends lots of time assessing whether prospective teachers have assorted bits of information, and very little time assessing whether they actually can create an education for the 40% of American youngsters who are non-Anglo and the 80% who are nonaffluent. In this chapter I suggest some ways that teachers might obtain the skill to teach those real American youngsters, and then I propose some goals for educators that go beyond their individual classroom skills.

### PERSONAL HISTORY

I grew up in a teeny house in an integrated, working-class neighborhood of West Los Angeles. My father worked at the Veterans Administration, starting out as a window washer and ending up as the supervisor of the warehouse. I realize now that he was relatively nonracist for a White guy of Irish background growing up in 1920s America. He read history, considered the Civil War a profoundly important piece of American history, loved the politics of Franklin Roosevelt, and hated the red-baiting of Richard Nixon. His political thoughts were confined to our home, until after he retired, because he felt constrained by the Hatch Act, which prohibited political participation by federal employees. His own childhood had been quite unhappy, and he was determined to provide a stable situation for his two daughters. Now that I know about the dinner table conversations many of my White friends grew up with, I realize that they received big doses of racial animosity to which I was never subjected.

My parents saved their pennies for a slightly bigger house and moved 15 minutes down the freeway to a different, Whiter part of Los Angeles just as I was about to enter junior high school. I was still a little girl, playing school and dressing up my baby dolls. My new classmates were going steady, making out at the movies, going to beach parties, and laughing at those who had not caught on to the social code. I had never heard of making out; we didn't have money for the clothes that might have made me fit in; and I found the social code a humiliating mystery.

On the surface, my misery had nothing to do with race—we were all White, and I thought I was just deficient somehow. But the monotone teenager experience of this suburb ultimately did rest on America's racial history. It is in suburbs like these that the sense of superiority, the isolation and entitlement common to much of White America, was constructed in the second half of the 20th century. And it is from this limited isolation that many White Americans are now escaping as they move back to the cities. The school choir and a church youth group saved me in high school. I discovered that I could make speeches and sing solos in public performances, which covered up great personal shyness.

I graduated and went to UCLA, an unhealthy place for a shy person, because a student easily could earn a 4-year degree there without ever speaking to anyone. But I caught little glimpses of the student movement and moved to San Francisco to become fully involved.

I learned a lot at San Francisco State—most of it not in the classroom. These were my biggest lessons: (1) Social movements do win sometimes and (2) the best leadership for American political movements often is provided by people of color. Open admissions, affirmative action, curriculum on the history of diverse communities, and a certain solidarity among Latino, Asian, and Black students were all won during that era.

So I moved from college to the work world a politicized person, expecting that I could join with others to make a difference and believing that the world of education would be a good spot for such engagement. I substitute taught for several years. This experience gave me fresh daily insights into racial discrimination, particularly the huge racial disparity between the teachers and the taught, and the awful overlooked problems that it caused.

Then I taught high school for 10 years at a very special public alternative school that came about as a result of the Civil Rights Movement. I had learned a bit about race from participating in the campus student movement, but any real racial and cultural competence I achieved came from the amazing Black and Latino adults who taught at the Street Academy. Bernard Stringer, Antonio Perez, Pat Williams Myrick, Pat Deamer, and quite a few others very gently taught me the two things I most needed to know—that I wasn't doing anybody a favor by collecting a salary for teaching "somebody else's children," and that Black and Latino teachers did not, by and large, have rowdy classrooms. I learned that rowdiness was not some natural quality of urban youngsters, but an unnatural product of schools dominated by adults who were very unfamiliar with urban neighborhoods and the youngsters in them.

I earned a doctorate at U.C. Berkeley and began teaching social foundations and teaching methods to new teachers. During that period I helped to organize many struggles around the composition of the teaching force, local control of school districts, multicultural curriculum, and so on. And to the surprise of many, these struggles were successful, at least on a limited level. For example, the two alternative teacher credential programs I helped to create with a colleague became the most ethnically diverse in the state.

## MY TEACHING EXPERIENCE

Teaching racial and cultural competence to the existing teaching force is only one dimension of the task before us as educators, but it is an important one. I am told by former students that my social foundations class had an effect on their racial and social consciousness and on their actions as teachers, and I believe that to be the case as I watch them in school districts around the San Francisco Bay Area.

While I am interested in the personal stories of my students, I do not begin discussions of race with their life stories, because I believe it gives disproportionate emphasis to racism as a personal matter. I begin with an objective look at the material difference between the conditions of White people and others in American society—a difference that is not apparent to many of us, even though we live with this difference every day. Having established that these differences actually exist, we are able to examine the history, the causes, and how we might address the issue as teachers. The most important aspect of my class is the reading and discussion of provocative descriptions of racial reality. This approach avoids several problems that are common to discussions of race: The non-White students are spared being looked to as spokespeople, the Whites are less likely to be defensive, and the teacher is less likely to water down the message in the face of student skepticism. I lead the discussion firmly, having established from the beginning that racial disparities are a reality, documented by a thousand statistics.

We read the work of Dalton Conley (2001), who points out that the accumulated net assets of the median White family are about eight times the net assets of the median Black or Latino family. This forces students to think about the fact that very few Black or Latino families are in the same social class as relatively affluent Whites, EVEN WHEN THEY HAVE THE SAME JOB. A Black teacher is very likely to have less wealth and property than a White teacher, even if they take home the same paycheck, and this gap correlates statistically with the gap in test scores between White and Black students. This can help to dispel the conclusion Whites often draw that their job is to correct something about the attitude or culture of the Black students, and can lead to thinking about our role in combating the injustices that result in this wealth gap.

We read W.E.B. DuBois's (1970) "Two Hundred Years of Segregated Schools," an astonishing 1956 speech that accurately predicted what would happen to Black students in the wake of integration. We read Vincent Low (1982) on racial discrimination against the Chinese in San Francisco schools, and we read a story by Francisco Jimenez (1995) on the school experience of migrant Latino children.

We learn that standardized tests were created by members of the Eugenics Movement and that many of the assumptions that undergird the tests remain unchanged (Sacks, 1999). We read some history from Tyack (1974/2007) and some research from Ladson-Billings (1992), and we read a bit from a book I wrote, challenging myths about urban school districts (Epstein, 2006).

We sit in a circle for these discussions, and I use activities that demonstrate the combination of structure and democratic inclusion that I believe the new teachers should use in their classrooms. For example, I create random groups, rather than having students choose their own groups, and I explain that this leads to greater comfort for students who are shy, isolated, or new to the school.

Many of the credential candidates do one-unit action research projects, and some of these have led to significant change. One student untracked the 9th-grade math classes at her school, so that all students were allowed to take algebra, for example.

## WHAT GOOD EDUCATION WOULD LOOK LIKE

I think teaching well is important, but changing the world for urban youngsters requires more than that. It requires active opposition to harmful policies and active engagement in the creation of better ones. Otherwise, each wonderful teacher becomes an inspiring exception to an otherwise miserable experience for many urban youngsters. We need an outline of the bad policies and a picture of what good education would look like.

### Changing Things #1—Who Gets to Teach?

Most discussions of teacher racial and cultural competence assume that the demographics of American schools will continue to develop as they have until now—increasingly globalized student bodies being taught by teachers who are mostly White, American, and female. The best manifestation of increased racial and cultural competence on the part of American teachers might be widespread and active opposition to this demographic disparity.

American teachers could create a movement to insist that Black, Latino, and Asian college-educated individuals be allowed into classrooms, earning a paycheck and being judged on fair measures of quality, such as the actual ability to teach the children who need teaching—urban, rural, multilingual, and nonaffluent children.

Is there any chance such a movement could take hold? Two developments make it possible. First, the United States is spending $7.3 billion annually to find and hire new teachers, because 500,000 teachers leave their jobs every year (Tucker, 2007). If we could show the country how to find the right teachers and help them to stay in the classroom, the cost effect alone might be an incentive for changed policies. Second, the whole population, including more affluent people, now has an incentive for making cities work better, a point made with great clarity by Oakland's new mayor and former congressman, Ronald Dellums: "People want to move back to the cities; so they are looking for policies to make them work." That could include policies to recruit and retain teachers who come from the most deprived communities, people who may be more likely to connect with the young folks who are now leaving school early.

### Changing Things #2—Allowing Children to Develop Academic Self-Confidence in a Developmentally Appropriate Way

Unlike much of the rest of the world, the United States begins formal reading instruction when children are really young. In Denmark, for example, children are asked to read at age 7. Because reading instruction starts in the United States before many children are developmentally ready to read, they may do poorly on standardized tests. When they do poorly on these tests, they and their parents are told that they must "try harder" and often they are retained or tested for special education. The result is hundreds of thousands of youngsters who feel less than competent by the time they are 7. An affluent family is able to intervene, keeping the child out of kindergarten for an extra year, sending the child to a less structured Montessori or other private school, home-schooling the child, or moving to a different school or district. Nonaffluent parents do not have these choices, and many low-income parents have had similar experiences in school themselves and so may not feel confident enough to intervene.

It is almost impossible to imagine the misery of a 5- or 6-year-old who is "held back" in kindergarten or 1st grade, but this is a common practice in the United States and a practice that we know leads to youngsters dropping out. The practice of holding children back a grade has become ever more frequent with the increasing emphasis on high-stakes standardized tests. By 2001, when the study was repeated, being held back was a greater fear than loss of a parent among the children studied. If I could make only two changes in U.S. education, they would be to change the demographics of the teaching force and to halt the retention of youngsters.

This scenario is more common for boys, who develop some skills more slowly than girls. The combination of diminishing confidence and inappropriate classrooms leads to youngsters being reprimanded, suspended, or held back. By 6th or 7th grade, it is easier to stay away from school than to go.

The most common proposal is to help teachers become racially and culturally competent. Although it is a good idea, it is nowhere near enough. If you make a child feel stupid at an early age, no amount of racial and cultural competence can rectify the situation.

### Changing Things #3—We Need a Program

Finally, teachers and others who desire more humane and racially and culturally competent schools need a program around which to engage the population in dialogue. The following 12-point program is modified from my recent book, *A Different View of Urban School: Civil Rights, Critical Race Theory, and Unexplored Realities* (2006):

1. Democracy and funding
   a. The federal government and business should have transparent and lessened involvement in educational decision making.
   b. The federal government could make its greatest contribution by lessening the enormous debt and facilities budgets of local school districts with the use of federal dollars.
   c. The major contribution of business to schools should be paying taxes in reasonable proportion to their profits and participating as interested partners.
   d. Every school district should have a fully functioning, locally elected school board. "Punish the victim" takeovers of urban school districts should end. If any district has an elected school board, then every district should have one.
2. Joy
   The current educational reform agenda does not mention the most important educational standard. Aim for joyful classrooms and schools filled with a love of learning and of young people, and for small, intimate learning communities, so that all students are connected to adults who know them well.
3. Bilingualism for all.
4. A multiracial teaching force that is representative of the national student population, of which non-Anglo (Latino, African American, Asian, and Native American) now total 40%. Preparation in racial and cultural competence and interactive teaching methods for all teachers.

5. Assessment
   a. There should be voluntary, nonpunitive parent/student evaluation of teachers. Teachers would solicit, read, and respond to anonymous student and parent evaluations of their teaching. These evaluations would not be tied to teacher employment or pay.
   b. Profit-making "blackbox" testing should end. Only transparent learning assessments developed by nonprofit organizations should be used.
6. Teacher development of curriculum, learning expectations, and lesson models with input from parents and students. Schedule the school day so that teachers can create, practice, and publish model lessons in each subject area.
7. Ending the torture of small children by returning to age-appropriate instruction. Examine models from other countries that have higher literacy rates than the United States and do not ability group, retain students in the same grade, or try to teach 4-year-olds to read. Based on this age-appropriate instruction, end grade retention and excessive, racially biased special education placements.
8. Reasonable college preparatory and life preparatory curriculum for all students. Create teacher-led panels to determine what all students reasonably can be expected to learn in high school, and then make these skills the college entrance requirement.
9. Taking the profit out of public education. End for-profit charters and other for-profit educational enterprises with the use of public funding. Move toward not-for-profit textbooks and materials.
10. School site power. Model public schools after the most elite private schools, and involve parents in genuine decision and policy making.
11. Hiring and contracting decisions that embody equity for groups of all ethnicities.
12. A personal advocate for every youngster. Each young person needs an individual to consult with throughout his or her education. This person would spot problems (e.g., several unexcused absences) and opportunities ("How about trying out for the youth choir?"); communicate regularly with parents or guardians; and listen with care

to the million issues, from drug use to college choice, that confront every youngster in this country. The Oakland Emiliano Zapata Street Academy provides a wonderful model in this regard (Epstein, 2004).

## REFERENCES

Conley, D. (2001, March 21). The Black–White wealth gap. *The Nation.* Retrieved November 15, 2007, from http://www.thenation.com/docprem. mhtml?i=20010326&s=conley

Du Bois, W.E.B. (1970). Two hundred years of segregated schools. In P. Foner (Ed.), *W.E.B. Du Bois speaks: Speeches and addresses, 1920–1963* (pp. 278–284). New York: Pathfinder.

Epstein, K. K. (2004, June 1). Miracle school: A child of the civil rights movement. *Phi Delta Kappan, 85*(10), 773–777.

Epstein, K. K. (2006). *A different view of urban schools: Civil rights, critical race theory, and unexplored realities.* New York: Peter Lang.

Jimenez, F. (1995). The circuit. In T. Lopez (Ed.), *Growing up Chicano* (pp. 137–146). New York: Harper.

Ladson-Billings, G. (1992). Liberatory consequences of literacy: A case of culturally relevant instruction for African-American students. *Journal of Negro Education, 61*(3), 378–391.

Low, V. (1982). *The unimpressible race: A century of educational struggle by the Chinese in San Francisco.* San Francisco: East West Publishing.

Sacks, P. (1999). *Standardized minds.* New York: Perseus Books.

Tucker, J. (2007, June 21). Replacing teachers who quit jobs in U.S. is a costly business. *San Francisco Chronicle,* p. 1.

Tyack, D. B. (2007). *The one best system: A history of American urban education.* Cambridge, MA: Harvard University Press. (Original work published 1974)

# CHAPTER ELEVEN

# A White Educator's Ongoing Journey: Toward Racial and Cultural Competence

## *Karen Manheim Teel*

> So much is wrong in this society, and so many
> people don't see it. My own, somewhat
> enlightened perspective, is often diluted, I'm
> sure, as I comfortably exist in a sea of White
> privilege. I find myself wallowing in that sea
> of White privilege, feeling like I am drowning
> in it. Then, I break through it for a few pre-
> cious moments. When I do, I have such a lib-
> erated feeling, but then I get dragged under
> again and feel like I am suffocating. One of
> my quests is to try to be able to articulate this
> struggle, pain, and elation.
>
> —Karen Manheim Teel,
> personal communication
> with Jennifer Obidah, 4/28/04

When I shared my state of mind about my Whiteness, articulated above, with Jennifer in the spring of 2004, I was a different person from the person I was before being mentored by her. My aware- ness of my White privilege and of the racial inequities in the United States had shifted dramatically from my thinking as a child and as a young adult. In my chapter, I walk down memory lane, conjuring up images of my childhood, of my early teaching experiences, of my amazing journey working with Jennifer in my middle school history classes, and of developing a conceptual framework for racial and cultural competence. This writing process has been a difficult one because I must describe my former racist self, a self that I am not at all proud of. The good news is that I believe I have evolved into a new self and feel liberated, and am on the road to becoming an ally and advocate for African American people, which is exactly the self I want to be.

## INFLUENCES ON MY THINKING

I have come to think of teachers with racial and cultural competence as teachers who embrace students from all backgrounds as equals and who work to understand, support, guide, and encourage them. I believe that becoming a teacher with racial and cultural competence is a lifelong journey, as Tarika Barrett and Pedro Noguera mention in their chapter. That journey was one that I began in 1993, when I admitted to myself that I had a problem—successfully teaching students of color who were primarily inner-city African Americans. I came to understand that my worldview and perceptions of those from different racial/cultural backgrounds from mine were rigid, arrogant, and condescending manifestations of the White privilege I was born and raised with (McIntosh, 1989). This mind-set was based on hearsay and lacked any direct, quality interactions with African Americans. This mind-set grew out of a complete lack of familiarity and knowledge of any cultures other than my own. Yes, I believe that I dwelled in what Ann Berlak refers to in her chapter as the locked door of the "adaptive unconscious"; I was an oblivious racist. As I reflect on my childhood and early teaching experiences, the influences on my thinking that resulted in my preconceived notions and stereotypes about African Americans become very clear.

### A Childhood Without Diversity

I grew up in an all-White neighborhood, in Fresno, California, in the 1940s, 1950s, and 1960s. My neighborhood consisted of working-class families in which the father was typically a blue-collar worker, and the mother was a housewife who often volunteered in the schools. My father was a liquor salesman who traveled up and down the San

Joaquin Valley, stopping at various liquor stores and bars along the way. Neither my father nor my mother graduated from college. My mother was a very well-read individual, though, and was always playing classical music on the radio or stereo. She was very passionate about music, theater, and art, and exposed me and my two brothers to European American culture whenever she could.

Growing up in Fresno, I never saw African American people except at school sporting events when my middle school and high school competed against the all-Black schools. Those schools were in some unknown part of Fresno, which we really did call "on the other side of the tracks." During my childhood, I was curious about the Black students I observed at the sporting events, but I assumed that they chose to live on their side of town, and we Whites chose to live on our side. I believed that we must have very different lifestyles and wanted to be with "our own kind." I never visited the African American community, and I never remember seeing a Black person in my neighborhood. It never occurred to me that Black people might not be welcome in the White neighborhoods or that White people might not be welcome in the Black community. I clearly didn't give any of this much thought.

As I went through my local elementary, junior high, and high schools in Fresno, I never had Black classmates, except during my senior year when one Black male student attended my high school. He and I rarely interacted, though, and it seems to me that no one paid much attention to him. He was a curiosity at best. During my high school years, my family and I watched TV coverage of the protests in the South that were an integral part of the Civil Rights Movement. Both of my parents supported an end to segregation in theory but never expressed much specific sympathy for the Black people protesting and never got involved in the movement. From a distance, they did admire Dr. Martin Luther King Jr.'s nonviolent protest approach, and my mother in particular articulated her belief in social justice.

In 1964, I graduated from high school and went off to U.C. Berkeley. I had noticed—when I visited the university before applying—that there was quite a diversity of students, including students speaking languages other than English. I remember being quite intrigued and excited about the differences that I observed. As it turned out, though, by the time I was accepted at Cal, there was no more housing available other than in sororities. I went through "rush" and pledged a sorority that didn't accept females of color at that time. Consequently, once again, I remained quite isolated from African American people where I was living most of the time. There were some students of color in my classes, but I never spoke with them. It wasn't until I got my teaching credential from Cal in 1969—and started teaching—that I finally interacted with African Americans.

## Early Years of Teaching

When I first started teaching students from different backgrounds from my own, I was a 7th- and 8th-grade world and U.S. history teacher at a junior high school in a large school district in the San Francisco East Bay Area. This school was located in a working-class suburb where most residents were White. The school employed "tracking" based on perceived ability levels, and I taught all White students, across a full spectrum from the lowest to the highest tracks, for a few years. Because of recent court orders mandating busing and the increased integration of schools, African American students from nearby inner-city areas began attending the school in the mid-1970s.

I was curious about these new students and asked the principal if I could teach one or two classes in which they would be placed. Before the school year began, the principal told me what to expect. He generalized by saying that these students had very low skills, were not motivated, and could cause me a lot of trouble. He suggested that I simplify my lessons, have very few class discussions, and do my best to keep the students under control. He warned me that they would not want to cooperate with me and probably would be a lot more disruptive than my White students had been. He urged me to send as many students out on referrals as I needed to in order to keep a lid on the class.

At that time, I did not think about the fact that all of the African American students who came on a bus to our school were placed in the lowest tracks. I assumed that whoever was sorting out the students knew what they were doing. Tracking made sense to me, given that students with similar skill, knowledge, and motivation levels had a lot in common. At that time, I believed that how and why these students were sorted the way they were just wasn't my concern. I remember being very strict with my African American students and having no trouble for the most part. I found them to be very enthusiastic and full of energy, which I enjoyed.

After teaching world and U.S. history at the junior high level for 10 years and teaching all levels of French for 4 years after that at the high school that my junior high students attended, I decided that I had many questions about motivation and the learning process— especially related to my White students—and that I needed to go back to school and get some answers. At that time, I honestly didn't believe that African American students could become more motivated. I had blindly gone along with the stereotypes presented to me by the administration, the media, and White colleagues and friends.

## My Doctoral Studies

In 1988, I embarked on a doctoral program in education at U.C. Berkeley. I was drawn to courses that dealt with so-called low-achieving students, and my professors at U.C. Berkeley focused on students of color and more specifically on African Americans. I read a great deal about the reasons why African American students were not achieving in school at the same levels as White students. The literature I read was written mostly by scholars of color, and their research findings and theories pointed to inappropriate curriculum and instruction by teachers like me (who were not familiar with African American culture and had biases toward their students) and to schoolwide policies based on racist notions and stereotypes (Boateng, 1990; Collins & Tamarkin, 1990; Hale-Benson, 1990; Haynes & Comer, 1990; Jones-Wilson, 1990; Oakes, 1985; Ogbu & Matute-Bianchi, 1986).

I became more and more concerned and outraged at what I was beginning to believe was the way that African American students historically had been set up for failure. I also became somewhat dismayed about how, as a teacher, I had been given the impression over the years that African American students couldn't perform on the same level as White students, and how I had accepted that idea. I realized that I probably did a great deal of harm to my African American students by having such low expectations of them.

During my first few years in the doctoral program, I was working on a research project dealing with how teachers learn how to teach reading in elementary schools and how they apply their learning in their first years of teaching (Hollingsworth & Teel, 1991; Hollingsworth, Teel, & Minarik, 1992). I visited many urban elementary schools during that time and was struck by the enthusiasm, motivation, and obvious intelligence of the young African American students I observed. What I was seeing was consistent with the literature written by scholars of color and others, but did not make sense, given what I was learning about the high percentages of failing African American students in our nation's schools.

## MY RESEARCH

During my research, I wanted to work with African American students because of what I had learned in graduate school. I had come to believe that the "low achievement" of inner-city, African American students was to a large extent the result of the kinds of teaching materials and strategies used by their teachers. I did not believe, at this point, that racist notions on the part of White teachers, including myself, might be a contributing factor.

With this perspective on the education of African American children, I collaboratively developed for my research alternative teaching strategies to test with African American students in a 7th-grade world history classroom. I was confident that I would be as effective using these alternative strategies with my African American students as I had been using more traditional strategies with my mostly White students in past years. These more innovative strategies were based on theories of school failure that I had read about in graduate school (Covington, 1984; Cummins, 1986; Delpit, 1988; Ogbu & Matute-Bianchi, 1986). My goal was to offer my previously low-achieving students experiences in my class that were both academically and culturally supportive.

The alternative teaching strategies were: (1) a noncompetitive, effort-based grading system that included an emphasis on effort, improvement, cooperation, participation, and quality of work; (2) multiple performance opportunities that took into account student interests and strengths, with assignments that included skits, art projects, oral presentations, simulation games, computer projects, creative writing, and group projects; (3) increased student responsibility and choice, including leadership opportunities for students such as serving as teaching assistants (TAs) for 2 weeks and choices built into assignments; and (4) book choices in a reading program that included validation of cultural heritage.

In order to recognize and celebrate cultural differences, I had a multicultural classroom library, which I highly recommend for all grade levels and all subject areas. Many of our students are not reading on grade level, and they need as many opportunities as possible to practice. They need time to read for pleasure in books they pick. My reading program consisted of 3 days a week, Monday through Wednesday, when my students would read a book of their choice for 10 minutes at the beginning of class. They were required to record their book and pages read on a 5 x 8 card, which they turned in every day. They received a grade each day they read, which was a strong motivator at first but wasn't that important as the students really got into the reading. Every Thursday, volunteers would give a 2-minute "book talk" describing anything they wanted to tell the class about the book. This was one of my favorite moments in teaching—when these volunteers became the teachers and talked, often eloquently, about their books.

For my research, I chose a different middle school, in the same school district where I had taught. This school had a predominantly African American student population, and I asked the principal to give me previously "low-achieving" students. During my research at this middle school, I documented a number of positive results with two different groups during 2 successive years. Many of my students were more motivated and performed better in my class than in their other classes, based on conversations with other teachers and on their report cards. I became convinced that these alternative teaching strategies were extremely effective in raising my students' confidence in themselves and in motivating them to work harder because they were experiencing more success in my class than they had before. However, despite this academic success, I encountered resistance from some of my students on a regular basis. Discipline was quite a problem in my classroom. Students often did not follow my rules, and many of them appeared to have very little respect for me. Sometimes the noise level escalated to the point of interrupting other classes.

I had not experienced these kinds of problems with my White students. I felt more comfortable reprimanding my White students and pushing them to achieve, reinforcing the attitude and approach I thought their parents used. With my African American students, I felt somewhat alienated from the beginning. I was confused about the ways they treated me and one another, and I was reluctant to seriously reprimand them for fear of being considered a racist and of becoming even more alienated from them. Unlike my perception of my White students, I felt I had very little in common with my African American students and their families. My knowledge of African Americans was based only on book, TV, and movie portrayals. I had no African American friends and had never even been around any African Americans for any length of time, so my discomfort was obviously based on lack of experience, preconceived notions, stereo-types, and hearsay. I did believe, however, that I wanted the students to succeed in my classes.

Coincidentally, during this time, I was hearing from both White and Black educators that White teachers might not ever be able to success-fully work with African American students because of their racial and cultural differences and because of the White teachers' learned, often unconscious racism. Initially, I rejected this notion because I felt so confi-dent about the innovative teaching strategies I had developed and about my belief in my students' potential to succeed. However, I was dissatis-fied with the high frequency of behavior problems in my classroom and with the strained relationship I had with a number of my students.

## COLLABORATIVE TEACHER RESEARCH
## WITH AN AFRICAN AMERICAN MENTOR

After receiving my doctorate in education in May 1993, I wanted to return to teaching the next year at the same middle school. My goal was to become as effective a teacher of African American students as I had believed I was with White students in the past. I was not sure, though, how to overcome the difficulties I had experienced with my African American students during the first 2 years I worked with them. After a lot of soul searching and reflecting on my dilemma, I decided that I either had to go back to teaching all-White students or had to seek guidance from an African American teacher whom I respected. On the recommendation of a White colleague in graduate school, I had observed Jennifer Obidah at my middle school during both the 1991–92 as well as the 1992–93 school years. Jennifer was finishing up her coursework at U.C. Berkeley in the same doctoral program that I was in. We had met there, and she got involved at my middle school, first helping out in an African American history course and then teaching her own self-contained class of students who had been removed from the mainstream classes because of "behavior problems." I found Jen-nifer to be a very effective teacher with these students, even with the so-called behavior problems. I approached her with the proposal that she come into my classroom to observe me and to give me suggestions on how to be a better teacher.

Jennifer and I agreed that she would observe the students in my two classes twice a week for the entire 1993–94 year. As a result of my apprenticeship and collaboration with Jennifer, I came to believe that my total ignorance of African American people and their cultural characteristics contributed a great deal to my students' sometimes disruptive behavior and resistance to me as their mentor. There was a barrier between us that was unclear to me before working with Jennifer. Jennifer has called that barrier "the ghost of racism."

I had to come to understand the nature of the barrier and then to recognize my own biases and racist notions that were contributing to that barrier before I could overcome it. Only then could I reach out to my students as I knew I wanted to, but couldn't. The influences on me as I grew up in an all-White community became clear. Jennifer guided me through a process of self-reflection about my biases that I had never recognized, considered, or confronted before. I learned that my ignorance and preconceived notions about African American people and culture led me to say things, react in certain ways to my students, use materials that were not particularly supportive of their culture, and design curriculum that was sometimes insensitive and offensive based on my students' history and culture.

This self-reflective experience was painful but the result was liberating—a kind of epiphany about how my perceptions of my students (as unconscious and unknown as they were to me) colored my thinking about them, decisions about curriculum, ways I reacted to them, and lowered expectations for them. I realized that I had been totally oblivious and clueless about the impact of these subtle racial and cultural nuances on my relationship with my students. In writing our book, *Because of the Kids: Facing Racial and Cultural Differences in Schools* (2001), I wanted to tell our story. I wanted other White teachers, experiencing that invisible barrier between themselves and their students (and colleagues and community members) of color, to learn how my collaboration with Jennifer helped me to confront what we saw as a racial barrier, to break through it, and then to become a more effective teacher for my students.

Without a strong rapport between the teacher and students, student success is undoubtedly jeopardized. As Jennifer and I pointed out in Chapter 1 of this volume, based on our own experiences, many teachers who work with students of color do not develop that important rapport between themselves and their students. We believe that this factor is the key to raising the achievement levels in our schools, and yet it is rarely discussed, much less explored and addressed.

My changes that did happen—at the end of that first year of our study and then into the second and third years—were very exciting and amazing to me. I became a very different person when I was with my students and their families, anxious to learn whatever I could from them about their lives, interests, customs, and dreams. I listened carefully to my students and nagged them to excel, which I had never done before. I wouldn't let them "off the hook," whether it was off-task behavior or below-standard performance. I became relentless and determined to encourage the best in them. I was no longer afraid. I talked to them about their college and career goals and referred to those goals throughout the year as I pushed them to achieve.

Whereas I had been a *passive* teacher before, I became a *proactive* teacher—an advocate for my students, pushing, pulling, nagging, and insisting on the very best each student could give me. I was able to reach many more of my students on a personal level, and I really believe that they came to think of me as a passionately caring mentor to them.

Another impact on me from this work with Jennifer was a feeling of anger, resentment, disappointment, and even cynicism about our country's unsuccessful efforts to educate African American students. I am still thinking about such larger issues and have turned to teaching new teachers who work with African American students, hoping my story will have an impact on them, too. As a way for me to continue to challenge my own biases and stereotypes, with another colleague at my university, I started a cross-racial book club dealing with racism and cultural differences. We have read and discussed a number of books such as Beverly Daniel Tatum's *"Why Are All the Black Kids Sitting Together in the Cafeteria?"* (1997) and Michael Dyson's *Is Bill Cosby Right or Has the Black Middle Class Lost Its Mind?* (2005). We have talked to our students about our experiences as members of this book club and have presented at an international education conference. This sharing of our perspectives about these sensitive issues, prompted by the stories in the books we read, forces each of us to look at, question, and grapple with our beliefs about racial and cultural differences in this country. I still worry about racial biases that are buried deep down in my "adaptive unconscious"—and the White privilege I was born with—and I continue to dig and try to unpack these biases so that I can see more clearly and continue to become more and more racially and culturally competent.

## MY CONCEPTUAL FRAMEWORK
## FOR RACIAL AND CULTURAL COMPETENCE

Since my work with Jennifer, in my role as a university supervisor
of student and intern teachers, I have developed a conceptual framework for racial and cultural competence that I have shared with these
teachers. I see racial and cultural competence as a continuum from a
total lack of it to a quite advanced level. I actually have been thinking
of the lowest levels of this continuum as a kind of "deficit model."
What I mean is that it's not the students with the so-called deficit;
it's often the teachers/schools/and system of education that have
the deficit in terms of demonstrating racial and cultural competence.
In designing my conceptual framework, I have come up with eight
factors that, to me, are key to all teachers' success with students from
backgrounds different from their own. These factors are:

1. comfort level with students
2. student academic engagement
3. personal connection with students
4. level of academic expectations
5. acceptance of responsibility for student performance
   outcomes
6. relationship with parents
7. self-evaluation/reflection
8. culturally relevant lessons

Each of these factors is important in and of itself, and, all together, they
can result in racial and cultural competence.

Given these eight factors, following are the characteristics of a
teacher I would consider to be at the lowest level of racial and cultural
competence—or "not competent":

1. is afraid of the students
2. allows the students to be off-task and even walking around
   the room
3. has no personal connection with individual students—
   knows virtually nothing about them outside of class
4. has very low academic expectations as demonstrated by a
   tolerance for off-task behavior

5. does not accept responsibility for lack of student engagement and success—blames the students
6. has mostly a negative, adversarial relationship with parents—not a positive team approach
7. does not self-reflect and evaluate his or her own effectiveness
8. seldom builds cultural relevance into lessons

Here are two examples of this kind of racially and culturally incompetent mind-set. These examples have everything to do with the teachers seeing only the students and their families at fault—and no one else, especially themselves—for off-task behavior and low academic achievement. The first example is a group of teachers, from two elementary schools, whom Jennifer and I spoke with a few years ago who recently had experienced an influx of inner-city African American students into their schools. After Jennifer and I described our journey together and suggested some strategies for successful teaching of low-achieving students, several teachers responded that they had already tried everything we recommended and nothing had worked. They said they were at their wits' end. Jennifer and I, of course, found this attitude very frustrating and troubling, although we had heard that pessimistic, negative response before. After our presentation, we talked to the principals of the two schools represented about the pessimistic tone during the question-and-answer period. Both of the principals attributed their teachers' attitudes to a grieving process their teachers were going through because of the loss of their White students and because of their memory of how wonderful it had been to teach them and what a struggle it now was to work with African American students. You can see that these teachers were at the lowest level of racial and cultural competence, given their preconceived notions and low expectations for their new African American students.

The second example is a beginning teacher I supervised one semester. During my observations of his teaching, most of his students had been off-task, either chatting among themselves, talking on their cell phones, listening to their CD players, or working on some other assignment. All the while, this new teacher proceeded with the lesson, ignoring all of these unengaged students. I saw students get up and walk around the classroom or even out of the classroom without the teacher noticing. He told me at one point that the reason that he wasn't more assertive and more demanding of the students was because he feared retaliation from them. He was afraid that they might assault him. Obviously, if teachers fear their students, they cannot be the kind of commanding authority figures and compassionate advocates that most students respond to.

In moving toward a more racially and culturally competent mind-set, I want to share a conversation that a teacher friend of mine had with the grandmother of one of her 2nd-grade students (Hollingsworth et al., 1994). As required by her school, this teacher had sent home results of standardized tests for parents to sign and return. Instead, this "parent" (the grandmother) came to the classroom with the test in her hand, showing her granddaughter had failed. This is what she said to the teacher: "What does this say about my child—that she's a moron, she's stupid and slow? Does it say that I read to her every night? Does it say that her mother is in jail and her daddy died just last year? Does it tell you that she's getting her life together slowly? Does it say that she's learning songs for Sunday school? Does it say she wants to be a doctor? What does this piece of paper say about my baby? I don't want it near her. She needs good things. She's had enough in her life telling her that she's no good. She doesn't need this and I won't have it. If your school can't come up with better ways to show what my child can really do, then I refuse to sign a piece of paper that says my child is no good" (p. 29).

As a result of this conversation with the student's grandmother, the teacher let go of standard performance and grade expectations and began to develop more personally responsive strategies and measures that helped her understand how to better improve her students' standardized test scores. I believe that these changes showed that this teacher was moving toward racial and cultural competence—into the levels of "somewhat competent" and "acceptably competent." The characteristics I see in teachers at those levels are:

1. not being afraid of the students
2. being more assertive, with better student engagement and students listening in their seats more of the time
3. making efforts to make personal connections with individual students
4. having higher academic expectations—becoming more demanding

5. accepting more responsibility for problems—not blaming the students as much and making fewer excuses
6. establishing closer and more positive contact with parents
7. being more reflective and self-critical
8. building more cultural relevance into lesson plans

When I reflect on the characteristics that describe highly racially and culturally competent teachers, I think of teachers such as the ones Gloria Ladson-Billings observed and described in her book *The Dreamkeepers* (1994), teachers like the ones that Jeff Duncan-Andrade described in Chapter 9, this volume, and student and veteran teachers I have observed myself as a university supervisor: teachers who

1. are very comfortable with the students
2. engage students all of the time
3. have a positive personal connection with each student
4. have very high expectations for each student and follow through with them
5. accept total responsibility for any student's lack of success
6. have a strong, positive relationship with all of the parents
7. constantly reflect on their practice and include others in assessment of their practice
8. develop and use culturally relevant lessons on a regular basis

## CONCLUDING REMARKS

Writing this chapter has felt like a journey to me in and of itself because I have tried to go down a path, exploring the meaning I have created of racial and cultural competence in all of its aspects and explaining my own quest to become a more competent teacher of African American students. I believe that our goal should be to raise our expectations and standards for all of our students and to make sure that teachers and schools are equipped to make those goals a reality. In order for this to happen, though, I believe that all of our teachers must become racially and culturally competent in the ways that I have described. There is so much to think about and so much action to take to make sure that ALL of our students in our nation's schools are receiving an excellent education.

**Note:** Photo of Karen Manheim Teel by Woody Teel.

## REFERENCES

Boateng, F. (1990). Combatting deculturalization of the African-American child in the public school system: A multi-cultural approach. In K. Lomotey (Ed.), *Going to school: The African-American experience* (pp. 73–84). Albany: State University of New York Press.

Collins, M., & Tamarkin, C. (1990). *Marva Collins' way*. New York: Penguin Putnam.

Covington, M. V. (1984). The self-worth theory of achievement motivation: Findings and implications. *The Elementary School Journal, 85*(1), 5–20.

Cummins, J. (1986). Empowering minority students: A framework for intervention. *Harvard Educational Review, 56*(1), 18-36.

Delpit, L. (1988). The silenced dialogue: Power and pedagogy in educating other people's children. *Harvard Educational Review, 58*(3), 280–298.

Dyson, M. E. (2005). *Is Bill Cosby right or has the Black middle class lost its mind?* New York: Basic Civitas Books.

Hale-Benson, J. (1990). Visions for children: Educating Black children in the context of their culture. In K. Lomotey (Ed.), *Going to school: The African-American experience* (pp. 209–222). Albany: State University of New York Press.

Haynes, N. M., & Comer, J. (1990). Helping Black children succeed: The significance of some social factors. In K. Lomotey (Ed.), *Going to school: The African-American experience* (pp. 103–112). Albany: State University of New York Press.

Hollingsworth, S., Cody, A., Dybdahl, M., Davis-Smallwood, J., Gallagher, P., Gallego, M., Maestre, T., Minarik, L., Raffel, L., Standerford, N. S., & Teel, K. (1994). *Teacher research and urban literacy education*. New York: Teachers College Press.

Hollingsworth, S., & Teel, K. (1991). Learning to teach reading in secondary math and science. *Journal of Reading, 35*(3), 190–194.

Hollingsworth, S., Teel, K., & Minarik, L. (1992). Learning to teach Aaron: A beginning teacher's story of literacy in an urban classroom. *Journal of Teacher Education, 43*(2), 83-95.

Jones-Wilson, F. (1990). The state of African American education. In K. Lomotey (Ed.), *Going to school: The African-American experience* (pp. 31–51). Albany: State University of New York Press.

Ladson-Billings, G. (1994). *The dreamkeepers: Successful teachers of African American children*. San Francisco: Jossey Bass.

McIntosh, P. (1989, July/August). White privilege: Unpacking the invisible knapsack. *Peace and Freedom*, 10–12.

Oakes, J. (1985). *Keeping track: How schools structure inequality*. New Haven, CT: Yale University Press.

Obidah, J. E., & Teel, K. M. (2001). *Because of the kids: Facing racial and cultural differences in schools.* New York: Teachers College Press.

Ogbu, J., & Matute-Bianchi, M. (1986). Understanding sociocultural factors: Knowledge, identity, and school adjustment. In California State Department of Education (Ed.), *Beyond language: Social and cultural factors in schooling language minority students* (pp. 73–142). Los Angeles: Education Dissemination and Assessment Center, California State University.

Tatum, B. D. (1997). *"Why are all the black kids sitting together in the cafeteria?" And other conversations about race.* New York: Basic Books.

# CHAPTER TWELVE

# Advice from the "Black Racist"

*Sekani Moyenda*

> Every society is really governed by hidden
> laws, by unspoken but profound assumptions
> on the part of the people, and ours is no ex-
> ception. It is up to the American writer to find
> out what these laws and assumptions are.
> —James Baldwin, 1996, p. 60

## MY EXPERIENCE

Be careful using my name as a reference. Since the publication of *Taking It Personally: Racism in the Classrooms from Kindergarten to College*, it has been a political and professional nightmare. When the book was released in 2001, Ann Berlak, the co-author and a White teacher educator, received accolades on her daring efforts to improve the quality of education for prospective teachers. For my contribution, I had the police call on me twice at my job, and there were literally four attempts to terminate my employment at my school. I couldn't open my mouth at work without a union representative *and* an attorney on each side. By 2004 it died down to the degree that a majority of the attacks came only from my principal. It most likely will not surprise most politically savvy people, especially African Americans, to know that a large number of those who opposed me and led the "anti-Sekani" campaign were indeed Black. Before I start giving advice to total strangers, I think it is important to share that I don't get off "scot-free" in this struggle for academic/cultural freedom within the workplace. Nope, in the 12 years of my career in education, any Black man or woman who ever was foolish enough to openly support me was professionally and, by White standards, quite effectively "nailed."

I call myself a Black educator. I promote and instill the African American-based skills and ethics necessary for African Americans to be successful in a racist society. I am an intellectual insurrection. I am a strong, powerful force to be reckoned with because I am competent, ethical, intelligent, and capable of learning from my mistakes as well as the ones other people make. I admit to my character defects (resentments and fears) and strive for progress, not perfection.

I work in the Western Addition of San Francisco. Here we deal with issues of addiction, gang violence, and poverty. The key word in that last sentence is *deal*. For those who live in the neighborhood under these conditions, the daily issues are simple because they are cut-and-dried. Managing debt is easy when you are used to having NO money. Shoot them or they will shoot me. I'm either going to have this baby or I'm not. The cops will show up when we call—or they won't. Life-and-death issues are easy to resolve when you constantly straddle a thin line between life and death. Everything in the middle, the grey area of life, is pretty irrelevant. There is little point in discussing college when you're not sure whether your 13-year-old son will live this week, since you started getting death threats on your cell phone whose number you have changed three times. Last night your 9-year-old would not sleep in his bed because the last shots that were fired landed a corpse under his window.

The contrast between that life and mine is that I live five blocks away from the killing zone, and my income makes it possible for me to pay the additional $100 a month it costs—now that I have added that to my insurance—to have my windows replaced every time someone breaks into my house. I get a "free pass," for now, because I tutor and feed my students and drive them home. Sometimes, I even baby-sit.

When a parent can't get back to school fast enough to pick her 6-year-old up from school and can't call because she is in court waiting for a decision from the judge, I either keep the child with me at school, take him with me to my doctor's appointment, or take him home until I get that call. I can walk through the group of young Black giant babies called a "gang" and say hello as I drop off their little brother or sister. I know many of them; I had them in my class. I maintain a respectful distance, pretending I don't smell the "dank"—a form of marijuana that is treated with other chemicals that make the high greater and the smell stronger and more pungent—so strong it knocks me back out of the front door.

I am flattered when a parent names one of her children after me, since that is the closest I will come to having children of my own. But, along with my education, finances, and "time served" at the same school for 12 years, living in the same neighborhood where I work affords me certain rights and protections usually reserved for those with "ghetto cards."

## EVERYTHING I NEEDED TO KNOW
## I LEARNED FROM 1st GRADERS AND VICE-VERSA

My behavior management plan in my classroom is rooted in social responsibility and justice. For me, it was confirmed as an effective approach during the hundreds of debates and discussions I had with people in the 5 years following the release of the book Ann Berlak and I co-wrote. The same valid questions (which I had been addressing all along) were raised about how to deal with the violence, addiction, and poverty that plague the Black and Latino community. I use an "empowered pyramid." I teach my students that they have all they need to be successful already within them. They have a heart with which to feel for others, a mind with which to think and plan how to do something right, and a spirit that speaks to them and lets them know when a situation is right or wrong. Their bodies are sacred and are to be used to "manifest" to the outside world all that is good within. Therefore, they must stop, think, and choose—but only after they learn to listen. Above all, they need ethical awareness.

### Student Learning Choices

My classroom is a laboratory of social justice. How can children fight for something they have never experienced? I tell my students all the time that I am not nice, but I am fair. Being nice is a privilege I cannot afford in the performance of my duty to teach. I will have to say and do things they are not going to like because my first responsibility is to prepare them to be the men and women nature intended—not to accommodate the impulses of a 6-year-old. I ask the whole class with kindness and respect the first time. I remind them the second time that I was kind and respectful, and I'm not getting the right response. For my little "thuglets" (the name I have given jokingly and most lovingly to my most difficult students), I explain that their day can be experienced on one of four levels.

*Fun Learning.* This level is a privilege to be earned, since it takes a considerable amount of resources to make dreams come true. Those who earn this level are the "old souls." They are the students who sit there quietly when insanity breaks out. They always finish their homework and participate in class in the most appropriate manner.

*Easy Learning.* They just listen while I tell them or read the answer and they write it down.

*Hard Learning.* A natural process that comes with making mistakes, using their internal resources, retaining the answers I already gave, and utilizing them in the form of classroom assignments, classroom behavior, and homework. Learning is the development of intelligence, among other important characteristics that intrinsically come with their own rewards, if they are willing to work hard. I reinforce a basic work ethic I am proud of—"fairly earn what you get."

*Painful Learning.* Positive reinforcement does not work on faithless children. Usually referred to as "at-risk" children, I define them as faithless because they don't believe doing the right thing, the right way, for the right reason, at the right time will get them the RIGHT result. Therefore, I have to manufacture a consequence that teaches the importance of working HARDER. Ultimately, painful lessons are the ones where a child gets no payoff from tantrums and unhealthy defiance. In my class, these behaviors not only bring no payoff, but they result in lost privileges.

## Five Empowering Characteristics

The problem and the answer are implemented the same way, with a twist to modify them to the specific needs of the child. But in general we start with the five empowering characteristics these students must learn in order to grow up and to be soldiers for justice.

*The Power of Faith.* They must be willing to submit to what is right and believe that even though they will not get what they want (a privilege), they will get what they need (a right). This level is called "strong spirit." Our motto is: "It's not my fault, but it is my problem."

*The Power of Independence.* They learn how to take care of their own personal needs. This is critical in 1st grade because they have to learn that they have the power to "do it by themselves"—an important developmental milestone. They learn that they are responsible for first solving the problems that go along with THEIR responsibilities. Learn to take care of yourself the right way, and it is easy to understand why it might be hard for others when they mess up. This level is called "independence." The motto is: "I have a good heart, a good mind, and a voice that tells me the truth. I can do it myself. When it's hard, we try harder!"

**The Power of Ethical Reasoning.** My classroom management system is rooted not in a child's ability to follow the rules, but in his or her ability to build and maintain a relationship built on trust. I don't care what you say, I care what you do. If you have done your classwork and homework, and behaved in a fair, kind, and respectful manner to myself, your peers, and our property, you finally have earned the privilege of recess, free time, and access to fun stuff in the room that belongs to the teacher. This level is called "trustworthiness," and the motto is: "Stop—Think—Choose."

**The Power of Forgiveness.** This is a critical step in dealing with conflict. It's easy to demand justice for oneself, but are you willing to give it even when you are wrong or you can't have something you want? What did they say or do that hurt you? Did you explain why it hurt? Did you ask for what you want instead? Did you give the other person a way to make amends? Can you let it go? These students get the prize box and the right to decide HOW they want to learn. I let them talk when all others have to be quiet. When the rest of the class is in trouble, they get to be free. This level is "honor." The motto is: "How can I help?"

**The Power of Wisdom.** There are always "old souls" in the class. They scare me. They should never be forgotten, but respected. These children are always reminded that they were better human beings at 6 than I am at 46. They get to decide which rules they want to follow and which ones they don't. They get to make the rules, and I give them what they need—freedom to choose what is best for them. They sit where they want, they play with what they want, wear what they want, and, when I lose my mind in class and I cloud up and rain on them, I always apologize to the socially and academically mature children who are patient not only with other students but with me as well.

The level is "wisdom." The motto is: "I am a part of the solution—not the problem."

That is my level system, which is value-based and maintained through our relationship to one another. It sits on my wall with clothespins with each student's name on it. Their level determines their status in the room. Irritating me with the same problem costs them privileges. Punishing me with tantrums and open defiance loses them privileges, and if that behavior persists, it results in a call home. Oh no, I don't do suspensions. I call home so the child stays after school with me and remains with me until the work—which they thought all that drama was going to stop them from doing—gets done. If they show off to their friends, I see a totally different side when I see them by themselves after school and they realize there is no audience. Substitute teachers don't handle behavior issues this way. I just leave my number so I can handle it over the phone or when I get back.

## MY FRUSTRATIONS AND
## MY CLEAR PRIORITIES AS A BLACK TEACHER

The only time most White people want my advice is when they can't deal with faithless children. I may spend the whole year proving I am not only righteous but I deserve and have earned their trust— now earn MINE. The other teachers consider these students to be "the defiant Black children." They want me to be the "overseer" of our children. They see me hollering at my class, and they see how my students or the parents respect me. Of course, they foolishly believe that I get this kind of cooperation because I am Black. Many White teachers I have observed appear to be afraid of the students but can't admit it. They pretend they are not afraid and blame the students and others for their struggle. They want to avoid taking on any of the responsibility for the poor relationship they have with the students. They aren't interested in getting their hands dirty, so they want me to "fix" the kid and make him "act" right so *they* can remain the friendly, kind, and benevolent teachers.

This, of course, raises a serious resentment in me. I resent the fact that I don't get paid extra to make their job easier. The principal and the teachers—who want me to work with these kids—will never acknowledge that my success with these students (whom others throw away) comes from a frame of mind and a specific set of skills. Even when I draw graphs and maps, many of the White teachers I work with are hard pressed to follow the simplest instruction because they don't want to take ownership of the problem. The incompetent teachers use the misbehavior of Black children as a scapegoat instead of examining their own ineffectiveness. If all the Black children sat down and were ready to follow directions, these teachers might have little or nothing to contribute to the lives of other people's children except what the "scripted curriculum" in Houghton Mifflin tells them to say. They conform to the rules of our dominant society, and White privilege serves them well. White privilege is a tricky asset to enjoy. As long as everyone within the institution accepts White privilege as a norm (meaning it is given but never discussed), one gets lots of perks.

This is the key to addressing my own internalized oppression as a woman. I wanted, like most women on this planet, to believe that people would give me what I needed or what was fair simply because I needed it and it was fair. I earn what I have now, and I will fight to keep what I've got. I demand compensation—fair compensation—in the form of institutional power (like academic freedom) when I have something that others want. I am not your friend; I am a co-worker, and I want what I am due. Until a woman said it to me, I could not let myself admit it. Now I embrace it.

I had to resolve this resentment over time with these realities. First of all, my skills can't just be duplicated—they can't just be understood—you have to actually believe me when I explain to you what is really happening in the head of a Black child. So even when I tell you in this chapter what I do, you might walk into your classroom, try this stuff, and fail because there is no SAFE way to live a socially just life or to practice social justice in the classroom. It is by its nature a revolutionary act.

It just isn't in my nature to pretend to be something I am not. I could fake it up until I got my credential or was surrounded by Black people. I can pretend I'm listening in a college classroom and take a passing "B" grade. I can correct papers while I pretend that anything being said to me in another professional development staff gathering—given by a White well-paid consultant like Ruby Payne—is remotely pertinent to me. But as soon as I see a Black child disintegrating into a stereotype or a Black parent falling prey to her addictions as her child's academic and social needs are neglected, I can't bother with the White man's agenda. Either I can argue about it, or I can take the kid in my class and teach him the truth.

I've got an army of people from my community who understand what I'm trying to do. The politically conscious and competent middle-class African American, like myself, who has come back to communities like mine also gets it. I separate the crime from the criminal, and I don't confuse who these children can become when they grow up with what their parents are today. I focus my attention on meeting the psychological, emotional, spiritual, and physical needs of the children and their families in a way my authority as a credentialed teacher allows.

In an educational system where everyone bends the rules to suit themselves, I use my authority to bend them to my will and to the needs of my students. Like a bear, I fight to protect my cubs, and from 7:30 a.m. to 2:00 p.m. they are indeed mine—including the ones in other people's classes.

## BEST ADVICE I CAN GIVE

Of course, you are probably thinking—"I know I can use this on my students!" Again, I warned you that what I do won't necessarily work for you. What I suggest is that you try practicing all of these characteristics as a teacher, as you work toward becoming racially and culturally competent.

### Do You Really Believe Every Child Can Learn?

Based on what? Evidence? Well, you've already failed. All the evidence suggests that Black and Latino students do not and cannot learn. Either you believe statistics or you believe in the power of justice. If you practice justice in the classroom, doesn't it stand to reason that the Black child will succeed in your class? If that can happen, doesn't it start with faith in your ability to teach? Do you have faith that you can learn to teach a Black child who behaves badly, resists learning, and challenges your right to run your classroom? If not, where are you truly meant to be? Where on this planet can you be most effective? Do you have what it takes inside of yourself? Can you be molded, broken, and whacked, and still get up and keep going for the next 20 years? Prove it!

## Are You Self-Reliant?

Can you learn how to solve all the logistical and administrative problems that plague this profession? Do you have what it takes to do what you have to in order to get your students what they need in the classroom to feel that they have the best of what they need in order to be successful? Do you need to use the students in your class as snitches in order to keep order? When you stand up for your students, and the principal and co-workers ostracize you, and parents want you fired solely based on a rumor or a small mistake, do you have what it takes to get knocked down and get up? Do you have a solid and reliable support system in your life in the form of friends and family to reinforce your importance in being there? Are you able to articulate to an angry Black parent and/or a tantruming child why he or she should trust YOU of all people?

## Are You Trustworthy?

If a parent is addicted, are you willing to work with the individual to get him or her help, or are you the kind to make "anonymous" calls to child protective services because you don't approve? Are you willing to call child protective services on a parent you like who may be on the PTA if you believe his or her child is being abused? Will you teach your students to understand racism and how it operates? Can you face examples of how you have let fear and resentment fester into racism and interfere with your effectiveness as a teacher? If so, then you have earned the right to discuss with a child or parent how internalized racism or sexism interferes with academic and professional success. Do you sit in staff meetings bashing parents and kids? Do you defend people because they are right, or because of their color? Are you letting fear dictate your actions?

## Are You Honorable?

When you have a problem with a co-worker, do you go directly to the person in private and speak your truth and listen to his or hers? Do you work out an agreement and stick to it? Do you own your part when mistakes happen or do you just blame others? How rigorous are you in your honesty and accountability? Are you willing to defend the righteous even at the risk of your professional success? Are you willing to do the right thing, even if someone is looking?

### Are You An Activist?

Does your curriculum reflect a clear political position that reinforces and supports social justice? Do you modify your teaching style, even if it means supplanting the scripted curriculum so your students will be on grade level before you advance them to the next grade? Do you make sure your students have glasses so they can see? Will you pick them up from home or drop them off if it will get them to school? Will you make sure all your students eat even if the district says they are expected to pay but their parents don't give them any money? Will you talk to kids on the phone after school to help them do their homework? Are you willing to choose as a life partner only someone willing to accept the inherent nature of educational activism?

## RECOMMENDED BOOKS

As an academic, I am well aware I should be shuffling through my written piece and interjecting quotes from other writers' books to legitimize my right to write on this subject. I won't. I have no academic ambition to be a professor at a university, and if you honestly think sticking book references in between theories proves credibility in how to function in a classroom, I will jump into a debate with you any time. Instead, I will recommend some books that had a profound effect on me and that influenced the worldview I enjoy now.

### Healing Books

A teacher is a healer, so you better start working on your unofficial healing degree now. I didn't say medical—I mean healing the wounds you will find open and exposed that no one else will be addressing. You may be the children's only hope, so make it count. Do what you would be proud to say you contributed. Here are the books that influenced me.

**AA Big Book.** To understand how to treat people who suffer from addiction, I recommend the *AA (Alcoholics Anonymous) Big Book*. It discusses and explains what it means to be an addict and what it takes to overcome addiction. You can purchase one at AA meetings or online at AA websites. There is probably a bookstore with recovery materials as well. The *AA Big Book* will give you effective strategies on how to help a family plagued with addiction. It will help you to know how to deal with the moral ambiguity that children of addicts often suffer in addition to not having had the chance to develop their own moral compass.

*You Can Heal Your Life.* (Louise L. Hay) This is a spiritual response to disease. This book was important to me because many problems that plague me and my people are not curable by science yet. When I realized that there were so many life-threatening diseases in my classroom, this book helped me to take a more positive view of health problems instead of being overwhelmed by them.

## Education from a Social Justice Perspective

These three books were a great help. James Loewen helped me to confront my own racial idealism. Freire is simply a God! I always ask myself what he would do when I am trying to decide how to take a social situation in my class and turn it into a socially just one.

*Lies My Teacher Told Me.* (James W. Loewen) This was the first time I read a book that not only explained the lie, but documented the truth. I actually have built my curriculum from this book because there are very few lessons that are written for 1st grade that address the issues this book raises—but if I'm ever challenged, I just whip this bad boy out on 'em.

*Pedagogy of the Oppressed.* (Paulo Friere) This is my bible. To acknowledge that poor people know what they need education to do for them is a spiritual truth—divine intervention. While I was raised by a progressive educator, this was the first time a book defined for me the kind of educator I wanted to be.

*Surviving a Borderline Parent: How to Heal Your Childhood Wounds and Build Trust, Boundaries and Self-Esteem.* (Kimberlee Roth and Freda B. Friedman) This book explained a lot of the parents I am forced to deal with because addiction often causes abusive behavior in a parent. The strategies in the book can get you through difficult parent–teacher conferences when dealing with a parent who "creates chaos."

## Books That Present Certain Spiritual Concepts

*Holding Wonder.* (Zenna Henderson) This is a book of small stories about children and their power to believe.

*The Kin of Ata Are Waiting for You.* (Dorothy Bryant) I think this story was based on a real culture that believes dreams are a reflection of a different reality in which we all walk. It is about what a culture would be like devoid of any form of abuse. Nice idea, isn't it? Call it fantasy or science fiction—I call it a goal.

I hope you enjoy these books and that they are helpful. The last one, *Taking It Personally: Racism in the Classroom from Kindergarten to College*, is mine, but it's only for people who want to understand the serious nature of racism in the educational system without being condescended to like a retarded child. If you are one of those "sensitive" people, you won't like my section; but if you are into the academic voice, you'll love Ann's explanation. I think Black educators who are equally progressive and working right in the thick of it, and want to be affirmed, will like my section.

## REFERENCES

Baldwin, J. (1996). *Wisdom of the African world* (R. McKnight, Ed.). Novato, CA: New World Library.

Berlak, A., & Moyenda, S. (2001). *Taking it personally: Racism in the classroom from kindergarten to college*. Philadelphia: Temple University Press.

# Epilogue

*Karen Manheim Teel*
*Jennifer E. Obidah*

Our book's journey, telling each individual author's personal and professional life stories, has come to an end. We can only hope that our stories have inspired you, the reader, to continue on your journey toward becoming the most racially and culturally competent educator possible. Our purpose in putting this book together was to provide multiple voices of educators who have considered and struggled with the challenges of racism in America as it impacts our students of color in schools. Some of us have been targets of racism ourselves over our lifetime, and others of us are members of the White dominant culture and have been the conscious or unconscious perpetrator.

All of our chapter contributors have done a great deal of soul-searching in an effort to find ways to influence the current, unacceptable situation for many children, adolescents, and adults of color, especially African Americans and Latinos, in American schools. Our intention was to challenge all of you new and veteran classroom teachers as well as you teacher educators to stop and think about your beliefs and practices, urging you to compare yourselves with the exemplary teachers described by the chapter authors. The standard we set was racial and cultural competence, meaning successful teaching practices that manifest themselves in the kind of encouragement and support that lead to motivated, engaged, and high-performing students, no matter what their racial/cultural backgrounds. We would like to revisit three of the issues that are repeated by a number of our chapter contributors: the "ghost of racism," White privilege, and social justice.

# THE "GHOST OF RACISM"

Several authors described their experiences either as persons of color being treated differently from White people or as White persons becoming aware of their own racist attitudes and behaviors that they had been oblivious to until they closely interacted with a person or persons of color or noted blatant examples of racism in our society. For instance, Ann wrote about the "adaptive unconscious," which she asserts houses racism deep below the surface of privileged people, mostly members of the dominant White culture. Growing up Jewish, Ann had experienced racism and noticed drinking fountains in the South that were off limits to Blacks. Partly because of these earlier experiences, she started noticing inconsistencies in her students' claims that they had become aware of their own racist notions and were "cured" of them because of being in Ann's teacher education course at San Francisco State. Ann described observing, as a university supervisor, a female, White student teacher in the classroom and noticing that she was demonstrating racist attitudes with her students of color in spite of her alleged revelations about her racism. There seemed to be a disconnect between what that student teacher believed and how she practiced it. Consequently, Ann's perceptions of the adaptive unconscious began to develop.

Jennifer, in our book *Because of the Kids: Facing Racial and Cultural Differences in Schools* (2001), started describing the reason for Karen's mismatch (between what she said she believed about the students and the way she related to them in reality) as an example of the "ghost of racism." Jennifer also experienced this phenomenon while living in New York in her young adult years and while in graduate school. She wrote about the stereotypes used to judge her by store owners and by her professors, none of whom believed that they were demonstrating anything resembling racist behavior. They were simply "skeptical" of Jennifer's honesty as a shopper or of her potential as a scholar, given other experiences they had had or based on what they had seen or heard from the media.

Carl and Edward described firsthand experiences with the "ghost of racism"—Carl with his grandson, and Edward as a kid. We are talking about attitudes and behaviors that White people are oblivious to and that have a negative impact on African Americans and Latinos on a daily basis. The root of those attitudes and behaviors is what has been described as White privilege.

## WHITE PRIVILEGE

White privilege was referred to often in this book as a very clear and overwhelming advantage that White people have in American society from the time they are born. Just as with the "ghost of racism," the authors of color tell stories of being unjustly treated by Whites for no good reason other than their perceptions of themselves as being superior, while our White authors describe when and how they came to recognize their privilege. Jennifer's and Ann's tales of their White students' early attitudes, as they were becoming classroom teachers, help to crystallize the assumptions that go along with White privilege. Christine and Karen explained their awakening to the pervasive and destructive nature of their own White privilege. Kitty argued for strong opposition to White privilege in all of its societal manifestations, moving toward a more equitable system of education. Sekani recognized White privilege in her fellow teachers, who always blame the students for their classroom struggles and want Sekani to "fix" their students so that their job will be easier. This condescending and entitled attitude is another example of the privilege that comes with being White in this country. This privilege contributes to the many inequities and glaring inconsistencies in America's actual practice of social justice.

## SOCIAL JUSTICE

The ideal of social justice strikes us as the ultimate in the noble goals that any society can aspire to. In the United States, we still have a long way to go. Although historically this goal, along a continuum, was much further from reality than it is now, people of color still experience a lack of social justice on a daily basis. Several chapter contributors discuss the popular American vision (of the way people are treated equally in society) as a fraudulent vision. During and often at the end of their chapters, all of our authors described ways in which educators can evolve in their practices so that they will be agents of change and activists in the pursuit of social justice. Paolo Freire's work with oppressed groups in Brazil was referred to by Sekani, Tarika and Pedro, and Carl as an example of what efforts can be made by educators to transform the system of privilege in a society. Kimberly's description of the goals of the Black Panthers in

Oakland gives us insight into historical attempts by African Americans to bring about that transformation. Jeffrey's teachers all have demonstrated the characteristics of racial and cultural competence that move us ahead in the pursuit of social justice. All of our work with underserved and often misunderstood students, with new and veteran teachers, and with master's degree students clearly indicates a dedication and determination to foster a new kind of thinking that could revolutionize the disparities in American life if the movement we are trying to promote gains momentum.

## RECOMMENDATIONS

So what is needed for this movement to take place, leading to an educational experience for all students that maximizes their potential in our society? This is the compelling question that this book originally set out to answer, and, through each author's chapter, advice was given —often including substantive suggestions for change. We found that there were some common aspects of those recommended changes, on which we elaborate below. These six recommendations will, we hope, serve as guiding steps on the journey of educators developing their racial and cultural competence. We also wanted to offer suggestions for teacher educators to use in guiding preservice teachers, during the time they are in the teacher education program, to become the most racially and culturally competent teachers possible. Clearly, there will be discrepancies among teachers in terms of which of these suggestions are already being practiced. For example, some teachers may be at the stage of admitting that racial and cultural differences between them and their students affect the learning and teaching process in their classroom, while other teachers may not. Some teachers may be seeking help and trying new teaching strategies, while others may be only at the stage of awareness that there needs to be a change, but may be reluctant, for a variety of reasons, to begin the change process. We recognize that there are teachers who are already practicing some or all of these recommendations. We commend these teachers and hope that they are serving as mentors and allies to other teachers in their school communities. Our recommendations may act as a catalyst for some teachers to ascertain for themselves whether there is a need for a change in their teaching practices to incorporate racial and cultural competence. If they determine that there is a need for change, the recommendations outlined below can help teachers in their development of this competence.

1. Determine your level of racial and cultural competence
2. Find a mentor
3. Become familiar with the communities you serve
4. Partner with your students' families
5. Become knowledgeable about your students
6. Become and remain invested in your students' academic achievement

### Determine Your Level of Racial and Cultural Competence

Our first recommendation is that teachers compare their own classroom experiences and, in particular, their relationship with their students, with the descriptions of cross-racial and cross-cultural competence laid out by Karen in her chapter, and exemplified by the effective teachers presented in the other chapters. We believe that teachers must make every effort to continually develop racial and cultural competence for the sake of the students who enter their classrooms.

This challenge applies to all teachers who are teaching students from different backgrounds than their own. In particular, teachers and teacher educators who knowingly and unknowingly subscribe to notions of White privilege, have never had relationships with people of color, and are working with students of color may have conscious and unconscious barriers that prevent them from being the best teachers possible for these students. For example, these barriers include preconceived notions and stereotypical thinking about students of color and their families. These teachers will need the help of other educators of color or White educators who have worked diligently to become allies with and advocates for people of color. These educators of color and White educators have taken themselves through the process of becoming aware of their racist notions and working through them to become more enlightened educators. Most important, undertaking this process has to begin with a committed decision to stay the course, since the journey we describe is very difficult. To attempt this or any of the other recommendations will require some teachers to enter their "uncomfort zones," which Obidah (1998) noted are spaces where "the act of challenging long-held beliefs may be a challenge in and of itself" (p. 68). To this end, we offer the second recommendation.

## Find a Mentor

Our second recommendation is that teachers pair up with a mentor in the process of developing racial and cultural competence. This mentor should be an educator of color or a White educator who clearly (as seen in his or her practice) has continued the process of developing his or her own racial and cultural competence. The mentor and teacher should consult with each other both inside and outside of the classroom, as Jennifer and Karen did. This partnership should be professional but also personal to the extent that the teacher can use this relationship to learn more about the mentor's interactions with communities of color outside of a professional setting. The mentors can assist the teacher to develop high academic expectations for every single student in the teacher's classroom. Essentially, this relationship is about becoming committed partners for social change.

## Become Familiar with the Communities You Serve

A third important recommendation is that teachers become familiar with the communities surrounding the schools at which they teach. Urban centers of metropolitan cities often suffer from debilitating social conditions such as economic instability, leading to high unemployment rates and limited employment opportunities. The impoverished circumstances arising out of this situation result in poverty and associated dysfunctions of substance abuse, crime, and violence. Inevitably, these conditions impact the lives of students and consequently the school setting. However, we contend that teachers should become familiar with their community because, in the worst socioeconomic environment, people live, love, care for their children, and want the best for them. Teachers cannot get beyond their stereotypes of what it means to live in such areas until they engage in what Solórzano and Yosso (2004) refer to as "asset mapping" in these communities: that is, finding out about the social networks and support systems that exist to assist community members in their struggle against their debilitating social circumstances. In considering taking on this challenge, Karen had to face the trepidations she had about going into her students' communities as a White person, given her preconceived notions about how she might be received. She imagined a possibly hostile environment where her life might be threatened because of what her Whiteness represented to the community residents. She assumed that even though she was a teacher who wanted to learn more about her students' lives outside of school, the members of the community would not welcome her among them. To assist teachers like Karen, some teacher education programs have now structured ways within the programs for students to connect with community resources through an unintimidating and mutually beneficial process. For example, preservice teachers are encouraged to pair up and visit churches, which are, in turn, prepared to receive them. In another project, to learn more about community networks that exist, preservice teachers are required to interview the elders in the community to learn how the community has changed over the lives of the citizens. These are examples of racial and cultural exchanges that can result in more racially and culturally competent teaching.

### Partner with Your Students' Families

Our fourth recommendation is that—in the K–12 context—teachers team up with their students' parents or guardians to support and guide the students' learning process. Teacher educators should underscore with preservice teachers the importance of building such a collaboration with their students' families. When teachers and their students' families act as a team, the students receive a united message of high expectations and encouragement to work up to their potential, allowing for no excuses. When this teamwork does not exist, students have a higher potential of academic pitfalls.

### Become Knowledgeable About Your Students

Our fifth recommendation is that teachers develop a greater understanding of the growing diverse populations of students attending urban public schools. This knowledge should encompass, among other things, students' history, culture, and language—especially when students' languages are in any way different from the language that is standard to the schooling process. Importantly, teachers also should try to gain a better understanding of the realities of students' lives outside of school. Taken together, this knowledge can assist teachers in making their teaching practices and, in particular, curricular activities more obviously relevant to students. In terms of curricular efforts, teachers can find themes of comparison and contrast between sets of knowledge. Teachers can gain such knowledge by doing as much research as possible (e.g., talking to people, library research, etc.). Teachers also can engage students in challenging textbook knowledge that presents biased views of different groups of people. In effect, whether we as teachers choose to accept it or not, students' lives come with them to school, and, as we have advocated in all of our work, instead of wishing for other students, teachers should prepare themselves to effectively teach the students they have.

### Become and Remain Invested in Your Students' Academic Achievement

Our sixth and final recommendation is for teachers to recognize and nurture their students' strengths, talents, interests, and overall sense of identity. Teachers should offer their students multiple performance opportunities through which to excel. Allowing students to succeed, in turn, builds in them the desire to challenge their weaker skills and subject areas. In addition, teachers should know their students' dreams for the future (i.e., their college and career aspirations) and continually encourage them to pursue these life goals.

### FINAL COMMENTS

Our assumption, when writing this book, was that all educators want to be the best teachers possible for all students. All of the authors in this volume have indicated their belief that many students of color, especially African Americans and Latinos, often have not been understood and supported by the teaching population in American schools (mostly middle-class, White women) and have been dealt with and taught inappropriately, given their cultures and other characteristics that do not necessarily conform to middle-class, White student attitudes and behaviors.

Our joint belief is that classroom teachers cannot shirk their responsibility to educate, with equal passion and dedication, every child who comes through their door. Because each child comes in with a different personality and a different set of childhood experiences, each child will need some level of individual attention.

We teachers have a moral obligation to educate all children in this country. In order to successfully achieve such a critical and noble goal, we all must take it upon ourselves to become racially and culturally competent—no matter what it takes. We must be committed to knowing our students both inside and outside of the classroom and committed to providing them with the skills and knowledge that they need in order to be successful in their adult lives. We cannot accept defeat. If we are failing, we must have the courage, determination, and fortitude to first admit our failure, and that we are to a great extent responsible for that failure, and then become researchers and change agents on our students' behalf. This may require extra time and energy outside of the classroom, orchestrating changes in ourselves and in the school culture and approach, and becoming more familiar with our students in their communities.

We will need allies in our particular context, who should include the staff, teachers, administrators, parents, and students. Our students are our clients and the recipients of the classroom experience we offer to them. It must be a group effort—with our students playing a key role—to create the most appropriate learning environment for all of our students. We have no choice. The future of all of our students and our society as a whole depends on it.

## REFERENCES

Obidah, J. (1998). Black-mystory: Literate currency in everyday schooling. In D. E. Alvermann, K. A. Hinchman, D. W. Moore, S. F. Phelps, & D. R. Waff (Eds.), *Reconceptualizing the literacies in adolescents' lives* (pp. 51–71). Mahwah, NJ: Erlbaum.

Obidah, J., & Teel, K. (2001). *Because of the kids: Facing racial and cultural differences in schools.* New York: Teachers College Press.

Solórzano, D. G., & Yosso, T. J. (2004). From racial stereotypes and deficit discourse toward a critical race theory in teacher education. In W. De La Torre, L. Rubalcalva, & B. Cabello (Eds.), *Urban education in America: A critical perspective* (pp. 67–81). Dubuque, IA: Kendall/Hunt.

# About the Contributors

**Tarika Barrett** is currently pursuing a Ph.D. in Teaching and Learning at New York University, focusing specifically on the dynamics of teacher community in high schools. Prior to this, she taught Deaf and Hard of Hearing high school students in New York City for 5 years after earning her MA from Teachers College, Columbia University.

**Ann Berlak** has been grappling with the challenge of teaching for social justice since 1961. She taught elementary school in Massachusetts and California, was a teacher educator at Webster University in St. Louis for 20 years, and now teaches in the Department of Elementary Education at San Francisco State University.

**Jeffrey M. R. Duncan-Andrade** is Assistant Professor of Raza Studies and Education Administration and Interdisciplinary Studies, and Co-Director of the Educational Equity Initiative at San Francisco State University's Cesar Chavez Institute (http://cci.sfsu.edu/taxonomy/term/28). In addition to these duties, he teaches a 12th-grade English literature class at Oasis High School (Oakland, CA), where he continues his research into the uses of critical pedagogy in urban schools.

**Kitty Kelly Epstein** combines activism with teaching, writing, and hosting a radio program. She taught at the Emiliano Zapata Street Academy, earned a doctorate at U.C. Berkeley, taught teachers and graduate students, campaigned for a more diverse teaching force, and helped to lead a successful grassroots campaign for an education-friendly mayor in Oakland.

**Edward Fergus** has worked as a social studies teacher, program evaluator, youth development worker, and researcher, focusing on the dimensions of racial/ethnic identification and academic variability among racial/ethnic minority groups. Currently he is the director of research and evaluation at the Metropolitan Center for Urban Education at New York University's Steinhardt School of Education.

**Carl A. Grant** is Hoefs-Bascom Professor of Teacher Education at the University of Wisconsin–Madison. He is a past-president of the National Association for Multicultural Education and a former public school teacher.

**Kimberly Mayfield** has been an educator for almost 20 years, focusing primarily on special education and multicultural education. Presently she is a professor in the Graduate Education department at Holy Names University, where she coordinates the Education Specialist Mild/Moderate credential program and actively works to bring more racial and ethnic diversity into the teacher pool.

**Sekani Moyenda** is a social justice educator, writer, and activist in the San Francisco Public School System. She is also the co-author of *Taking It Personally: Racism in Education from Kindergarten to College.*

**Pedro A. Noguera** is a professor of Sociology at New York University and the Executive Director of the Metropolitan Center for Urban Education. He is also the author of the award-winning book *City Schools and the American Dream.*

**Jennifer E. Obidah** is currently the Director of the Education Evaluation Centre at the University of the West Indies, Cave Hill Campus, Barbados. She lives in Barbados with her 3-year-old daughter, Emike Jewel Obidah.

**Christine Sleeter** is Professor Emerita in Teacher Education at California State University–Monterey Bay. A widely published author, her teaching and research have focused on antiracist multicultural education and teacher education.

**Karen Manheim Teel** has been an educator for almost 40 years, focusing her teaching and writing in recent years on teacher research, urban education, and the impact of racial and cultural differences on teaching and learning. Currently she is a professor in the Graduate Education Department at Holy Names University in Oakland, California, where she teaches, supervises Single Subject credential students, and works with Master's students.

# Index